Preface

Golf is truly a lifetime sport and a wonderful game. It challenges us, both mentally and physically, and serves as a great way to relieve stress amongst some of the most beautiful scenery one can imagine. Golf is more than a game; it's a journey. Along the way we develop lifelong friendships, learn much about responsibility, commitment, the benefits of hard work, and more than anything else, ourselves. The game can and should provide each of us with a lifetime full of enjoyment.

The purpose of this book is to provide beginners, intermediate players, and advanced players with the simple fundamentals necessary to play the game of golf. It also provides students with a much-needed look at other areas of the game. Understanding terminology, the history, learning good etiquette, the basic rules, scoring, and a little about equipment is instrumental in becoming a good golfer. This book addresses both the mental and physical aspects of the game, the right and wrong way to practice, playing competitively, a little about college recruiting, and yes, even how to swing a golf club.

The golf swing is simple; often times it is made difficult only due to a lack of understanding. There are literally thousands of books and tapes developed each year to help people play better golf and yet the national average handicap for a male is within a stroke of what it was 30 years ago. In spite of all the advances in equipment we have not improved. The reason is simply, there is no secret swing or method that's going to help you play better. You must develop good fundamentals. Every swing fault is a result of poor fundamentals. With good fundamentals and practice anyone can learn to play and enjoy this game.

We hope that this book will make the learning process easier, the game more fun, and send you on your way to a lifetime of enjoyment-good luck and play well.

William R. Lamb & Jon Antunes

Acknowledgements

With each new book, I am reminded of how much I have benefitted from golf and how blessed I am to have been introduced to the game some 30 years ago by my brother-in-law Mark Johnson. Since that time golf has played a huge role in my life-thanks Mark. So many people in each of our lives have helped us to get where we are and more times than not we forget to say thanks. I was introduced to golf at age 20. At that time in my life I had a ninth grade education and had been living on my own since age 15. I now possess a bachelors degree in Mathematics from the University of Mary Hardin Baylor as well a masters degree from Baylor University. I own the country club where I once served as a bagboy and have a wonderful family. A special thanks to my Uncle Ray and Aunt Connie for looking out for me while I was young and on my own. Also thanks as well Uncle Ray for the wonderful sketches in this book. I would like to thank my wife's parents Bob and Bonnie Johnson for their encouragement in getting me back in school, my wife for allowing us to be poorer than poor while I received my education, and my coach Mac Hickerson for giving me a chance to attend college and play golf. I could barely break 80 when coach Hickerson took me into the golf family at the University of Mary Hardin Baylor. Special thanks to my good friend Charlie Norris-(a two-time Oklahoma state representative), who worked for five years with me when I started my first golf academy and would never take a penny of pay. I'd like to thank the game of golf for challenging me, helping me to grow as a person, giving me a purpose, and profoundly changing my life. Thanks as well to the greatest teaching partner in the world Jon Antunes. I'm blessed to have Jon as a partner and as a friend. Thank you also to Baylor assistant coach Jordan Cox, former McLennan coach Bob Ammon, McLennan Girls coach Stan Mitchel, and China Spring coach Tommy Billeaud for their input. A big thank you to our sponsor Nike Golf as well. Most of all I thank God for the many blessings I've received throughout my life. "I can do all things through Christ who strengthens me." Philippians 4:13

William R. Lamb

I would like to thank God for giving me the opportunity to acquire the knowledge necessary in my life to write this book. I would also like to thank my dad for teaching me the game of golf and for teaching me to love it as well. I would like to thank all of my current and past students who have worked so hard at the game of golf. It has been a pleasure to watch you grow. I would like to thank my wife for helping me find the time to write this book. Last of all, I would like to thank my two year old daughter Hannah for not hitting the delete button on the computer.

Jon Antunes

Golf 101

Let the Journey Begin

William R. Lamb, PGA Professional

Jon Antunes

Kendall Hunt
publishing company

www.kendallhunt.com
Send all inquiries to:
4050 Westmark Drive
Dubuque, IA 52004-1840

Table of Contents

History of the Game

History of the Game

Although the roots of golf are not totally clear it is believed the game originated in Scotland. Scottish Sheppard's, using their crooks to knock pebbles into small holes in the ground thousands of years ago, are credited with being the first to play. Others believe that the game began in Holland. Legend has it that mentally ill patients who were institutionalized in Holland were given sticks to knock around small rocks during their time outside. This kept them busy and provided them with exercise. While trading with Scotland across the North Sea, the Dutch would show the Scots this game and then quietly make fun of the Scots for acting like the mentally ill patients back home. Being mentally ill is not a pre requisite for playing golf; however at times it can be considered an asset. The first documented evidence of the game in Scotland was in the 15th century. King James II prohibited golf because it detracted from the skill of archery, and at that time the defense of the country depended greatly upon expertise with bow and arrow. King James IV ascended to the throne in 1500 and became interested in the game and soon opposition disappeared. Mary, Queen of Scots, is thought to be the first woman to play the game.

Over the ensuing years many golf organizations and groups began to appear. Golf as a sport evolved in the mid 18th century when the St. Andrews Society of Golfers was formed and the first rules were written. Those 13 rules are still the nucleus of the rules we use today. In 1884 the Society became the famous Royal and Ancient

Golf Club of St. Andrews. The course at St. Andrews originally had 22 holes but was later shortened to 18.

The first tournament played was the British Open held in 1860 at the St. Andrews course. The open is still played today and is designated as one of the four major championships on the PGA tour. The others are the Masters, the US Open, and the PGA Championship. Twenty-five years after the first British Open tournament was held, the first British amateur championship was completed.

A Scot named John Ried introduced golf to the United States in 1888. Ried and his neighbors played the game on a three-hole course and shared a single set of clubs. The first recognized US golf course to be built was in Yonkers, New York in 1888.Four years later Shinnecock Hills, also in New York, was built and became the first organized golf club in the United States as well as the first to build a clubhouse. Golf historians are unclear as to where the first 18-hole course was built in the United States. It is believed that the Chicago Club in Illinois may have been the first to be built when Blair McDonald, an American who went to school in Scotland, enlarged the club from 9 to 18 holes in the late 19th century. The game began to grow and the first public golf links were built in New York City just before the turn of the century. From that time forward golf became a sport available to all classes of people, although early on it was enjoyed mostly by the wealthy.

The **USGA** (United States Golf Association) was formed in1895. Its purpose was to serve as the official caretaker of the game. Responsibilities included growing the game, testing and controlling new equipment, and enforcing and revising the rules, as well as ensuring the integrity of the sport. That same year the USGA conducted three tournaments, the US Amateur, the US Open for men, and the US Open for women. It took 16 years for an American to win the US Open. In 1911 Johnny McDermott became the first to do

Bobby Jones

so. Two years later in 1913 Francis Quimet became the first American amateur to win the Open tournament. Later a great amateur golfer from Georgia named Bobby Jones won all four major tournaments in one year, (the British Open, the British Amateur, as well as the US Open and the US Amateur); a feat that to this day has not been equaled.

Francis Quimet

Another important organization, the PGA of America (professional golfers association) was formed in 1916. The **PGA** is the world's largest working sports organization with more than 28,000 members who are experts in growing, teaching, and managing the game of golf.

Golf is much the same game today as it was in Europe 500 years ago. The game grew at a relatively steady pace after its introduction into the United States until late in the 1950's when its popularity increased greatly. Players like **Arnold Palmer** and **Jack Nicklaus** caused increased television coverage, which introduced many new people to the game. Jack Nicklaus is still considered to be the greatest player of all time. Jack won a record 20 major championships and finished second 19 times. In recent years, however, players such as Tiger Woods and Phil Mickelson have made golf even more popular and with a much more diversified group of people. Mr. Palmer's charisma was a major factor in establishing golf as a compelling television event in the 1950s and 1960s, setting the stage for the popularity it enjoys today. Perhaps the greatest business relationship in the history of sport was sealed by a single handshake with Arnold Palmer and Mark McCormack. The multibillion dollar company IMG was formed and a contract was never needed, just a handshake to this day. The company is now an empire with 2,500 employees, 86 offices in 33 countries, and a client list ranging from Tiger Woods to Roger Federer, from the Kennedy Space Center to the Pope.

Golf today is perhaps the fastest growing sport in the world with more than 25 million people playing in the United States alone. Golf courses are found everywhere in the United States today. Not only large cities but also even the smallest of towns usually have their own golf courses. It is a game enjoyed by both young and old, male and female and is considered to be a sport one can enjoy for a lifetime. Golf's popularity has grown over the years for many reasons but mostly due to the fact that it places few restrictions on who can and cannot participate. It's a game that can be played by young and old, those who are short and those who are tall, men and women alike, everyone can enjoy playing the game!

Jack Nicklaus holing a putt at the 17th in the 1986 Masters en route to winning his 6th Masters Championship and his 18th professional major at age 46.

Arnold Palmer throwing up his hat after he won the 1960 U.S. Open Championship which was held at Cherry Hills Country Club in Englewood, Colorado.

Arnold Palmer

NOTES

Name _____   Date _____

Chapter Review

1. When was golf introduced in America?

    _____

2. Who introduced the sport to America?

    _____

3. Where was the first organized golf club in America?

    _____

4. Who was the first American to win a major and
    what major did he win? _____

    _____

5. What do the letters USGA stand for?

    _____

6. In what year was the USGA formed?

    _____

7. What is one purpose of the USGA?

    _____

8. When was the PGA of America formed?

    _____

9. Who is the only golfer to win all four major
    championships in the same calendar year?

    _____

10. List one reason why golf is such a popular sport.

    _____

11. Who is considered the greatest golfer of all time?

    _____

Terminology

Terminology

<u>Course</u>

1 Tee boxes

2 Tee markers

3 Teeing area

4 Rough

5 Fairway

6 Lateral water hazard

7 Regular water hazard

8 Green

9 Flag

10 Bunkers

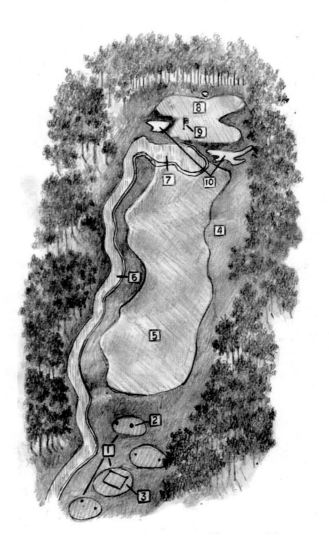

Tee Box	*Area from which you are required to begin play on each hole.*
Tee Markers	*Markers on tee box that define front boundaries of teeing area.*
Teeing Area	*Rectangular area in which the ball must be teed to begin play on each hole. The area is defined by drawing a line between the tee markers and another two club-lengths back.*
Fairway	*Closely mown area between the tee and the green.*
Rough	*Area that borders fairway, the grass is cut slightly higher than the fairway.*
Green	*Putting surface, which contains the hole. The grass is cut lower than the fairway.*
Hole	*Hole in the green in which the ball must come to rest.*
Flag	*Pole with flag that identifies where the hole is located on the green.*
Fringe	*Closely mown area around the green. The grass is cut lower than the fairway but not as low as the green. (Sometimes referred to as the apron or collar.)*

Cup	*Metal or plastic cup placed inside the hole to hold the flag.*
Lateral Hazard	*Area on the course filled with water. Lateral hazards are defined by **red** lines or stakes.*
Regular Hazard	*Area on the course filled with water. Regular hazards are defined by **yellow** lines or stakes.*
Bunker	*Area on the course that is filled with sand and serves as an obstacle. (Sometimes referred to as a sand trap).*
Out of Bounds	*Area around a course where play is prohibited. Always identified by white lines or stakes.*

Scoring Terms

Stroke	*Any attempt to make contact with the ball.*
Front Nine	*The first nine holes of a stipulated round of golf.*
Back Nine	*The last nine holes of a stipulated round of golf.*
Gross Score	*Your total score before your handicap is deducted.*

Net Score	*Your total score after your handicap is deducted.*
Birdie	*One stroke below par.*
Eagle	*Two strokes below par.*
Bogey	*One stroke above par.*
Double Bogey	*Two strokes above par.*
Par	*The score a skilled player is expected to make on a hole.*
Signature	*A mark made representing your name attesting that you kept the score and that it is correct.*
Scorecard	*A card that allows you to keep track of the score made by you or your opponent on each individual hole. It also has a place for the front nine score; the back nine score; the total score; and two signatures, yours and your opponents'.*
Lie	*The condition in which your ball lies after you have hit it.*

Improving your Lie   *The ability to pick your ball up and place it the specified distance from where it lies onto a better lie*

Playing the Ball Down *A rule requiring you to play the ball as you find it. You may not move it from the lie in which you find it; doing so will result in a penalty stroke and you will have to replace it.*

<u>Equipment</u>

<u>Club Terms</u>

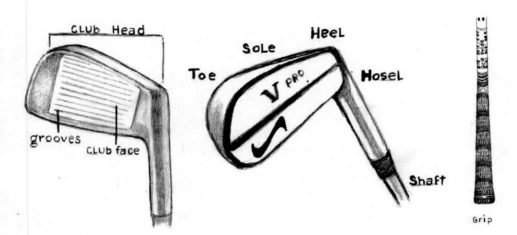

Golf Club   *Object used to advance your ball around the golf course.*

Grip   *Area of club on which the hands are placed.*

Shaft   *Part of club that connects the grip with the club head.*

Club head   *Area of club which strikes the golf ball.*

Club face   *Front of club head where the grooves are placed.*

Grooves   *Lines cut in clubface used to impart spin on the golf ball.*

Heel   *Area where the shaft connects to the club head.*

Toe   *Area of club farthest from the hosel.*

Sole   *Area of club closest to the hosel.*

Hosel   *Area of club where the shaft enters the club head.*

NOTES

Name _____   Date _____

Chapter Review

1. What is a score of one over par referred to as?

   _____

2. What is a score of one under par referred to as?

   _____

3. What term describes the closely mown area between the tee and the green?

   _____

4. What term refers to the area from which you are required to begin play on each hole?

   _____

5. What term is used to describe your total score before your handicap is deducted?

   _____

6. What do you call the area where the shaft connects to the club head?

   _____

7. What term is used to describe the score a skilled player is expected to make on a hole?

   _____

8. The ability to pick your ball up and place it the specified distance from where it lies onto a better lie is known as? _____

9. The area that borders the fairway where the grass is cut slightly higher than the fairway itself is referred to as:

   _____

10. What is the term that refers to two strokes below par? _____

How the Game is Played

How the Game is Played

     At first glance the object of the game seems relatively simple. All one has to do is to hit a 1.61 inch diameter ball into a 4.25 inch diameter hole in as few swings as possible. This is, however, where the simplicity ends. The reality is that the game is much more complicated than just hitting a ball into a hole. In order to be successful at golf, one has to take in to account the speed and direction of wind; the undulations of the fairway and greens; one must avoid sand traps, trees, high rough, water hazards, and out-of-bounds. Winston Churhill describes the objective of golf as "a game whose aim is to hit a very small ball into a very small hole, with weapons singularly ill-designed for the purpose". We hope that the following paragraphs will give you a better understanding of how the game is played.

     There is a starting point referred to as the **tee box**. On the tee box there is a specific area you must begin play from. This area is called the **teeing area** and is identified with markers called **tee markers**.

The teeing area is defined by drawing an imaginary line between the **tee markers** and another imaginary line that is defined by the length of two golf club and extends backwards from the tee markers. You must tee your ball up within this imaginary rectangular area; however, you may stand outside of the area as long as your golf ball is within the area. You may place the ball on the ground or you can place it on a tee, which is a small peg designed to hold the ball above the ground.

There are several sets of tee boxes on each hole. The set farthest from the hole is the most challenging and is usually referred to as the professional tees. The next teeing area is closer to the hole and is slightly less challenging. This set is usually referred to as the men's tees. The tees closest to the green are the least challenging and are referred to as the ladies' tees. A better way of defining the tees would be to call them the beginner, the intermediate, and the advanced tees. **If you are a beginner, man or woman, you should start playing at the front tees. As your skill level increases then you should move back to a tee that challenges you**.

Between the tee box and the **green** (putting surface which contains the hole) is the **fairway**. The fairway is a closely mown area in which you try to make your ball come to rest on your way to the green. An area of grass that is much higher surrounds the fairway and is referred to as the **rough**. The rough is much harder to play a shot from and should be avoided if at all possible. Throughout the fairway and the rough are areas known as **hazards**. Hazards are obstacles put there to add beauty as well as to make the game more challenging. Hazards may be in the form of **water hazards** (areas filled with water) or in the form of **bunkers** (areas filled with sand).

There are specific rules that apply when playing out of these hazards. These rules will be discussed in the rules section of this book.

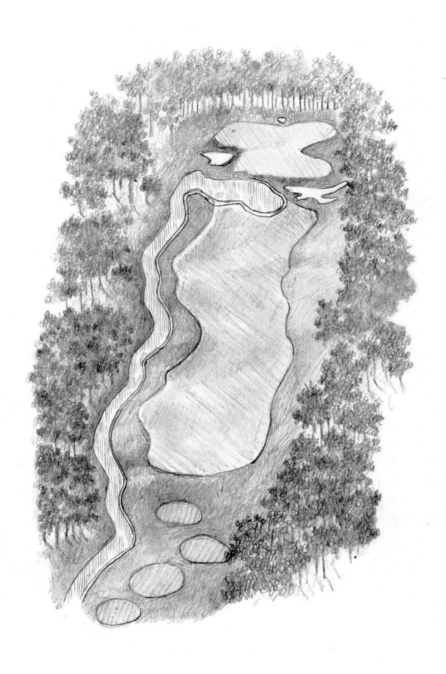

After you have hit your ball from the teeing area (we hope into the fairway and not into the rough or hazards), and have reached the green, you will find a 4.25-inch diameter metal or plastic cup placed 6 inches deep into the putting surface. A flag on a pole is placed in the cup so it can be seen from a distance.

An area of grass, known as the **fringe**, surrounds the green and helps to separate the green from the fairway.

When your ball comes to rest on the green you may pick it up for the first time since hitting it from the tee box. Never pick your ball up until it comes to rest on the putting surface unless local rules specify otherwise. Before picking the ball up you must mark where it lies accurately so that it can be replaced when it is your turn to play. When your ball is farthest from the cup you are said to be **away** and must try to hit the ball into the hole in as few strokes as possible. The club of choice should be the putter; however, you may use any club in your bag.

Your score is simply the summation of the number of strokes it took you to get your ball from the tee to the hole and includes any misses and/or penalty shots. After you have finished the first hole, you may proceed to the second hole. Upon finishing 18 holes, the summation of the strokes on each hole will determine your score.

The Equipment

The equipment we use to play the game consists of a set of golf clubs (irons and woods), a putter, balls, tees, a glove, shoes, and a bag to carry all of it. During a round of golf you may use any club for any shot that you may encounter. Sometimes this is a bit of a problem since you are allowed to carry 14 clubs in your bag. To choose the right club for a particular shot requires one to have an understanding of the clubs and their playing characteristics. Each club varies in length and in the amount of loft on the clubface. These two features, along with club head speed, are what determine how high or low and how far the ball will travel. The following pictures show how the lengths of the clubs and lofts vary.

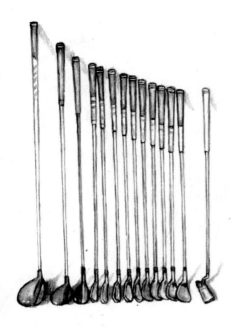

A normal set of clubs includes a couple of woods, some irons and a putter. **The longer the iron the smaller the number on the iron will be**. A 2-iron, for example, is longer than a 7-iron. The same holds true with the woods. A typical set will include: a number 1-wood, 3-wood, hybrid, 3-iron through 9-iron, a pitching wedge, a sand wedge, a lob wedge, and a putter.

As the length of the club gets shorter, the loft of the clubface increases. The result is that the shorter the iron the higher and shorter the ball will travel. The ball will travel higher due to the increased loft and will travel a shorter distance because less club head speed is generated with the shorter shaft.

The putter has little or no loft and is used to roll the ball into the hole once you have reached the green. The 2, 3, and 4-irons are referred to as the **long irons**. The 5, 6, and 7-irons are referred to as the **mid irons** and the 8, 9, and pitching wedge are referred to as the **short irons**. The number 1-wood is usually referred to as a driver and may be made of wood or metal. The number 2, 3, 4, and 5-woods are referred to as fairway woods. These woods acquired their name because they are normally hit from the fairway.

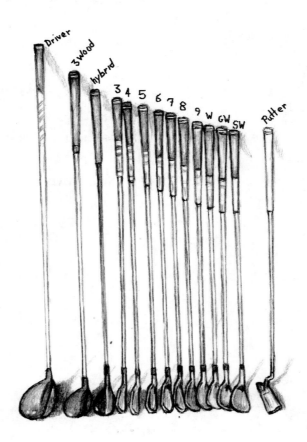

Range of approximate distances for average golfers

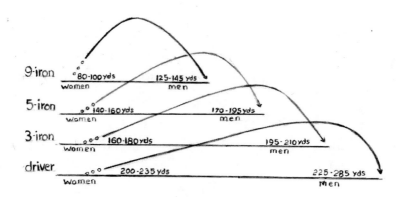

9-iron   80-100 yds   125-145 yds
        women   men

5-iron   140-160 yds   170-195 yds
        women   men

3-iron   160-180 yds   195-210 yds
        women   men

driver   200-235 yds   225-285 yds
        Women   Men

There are two basic club head designs. One is referred to as a **blade** and the other is a **cavity back**. In the picture below the club head on the left is an example of a blade and the one on the right is an example of a cavity back.

Cavity back clubs are usually termed as game improvement clubs. The weight has been taken out of the middle of the club and redistributed around the perimeter. This makes the club more forgiving on off-center hits and makes it easier to get the ball up in the air with the long irons.

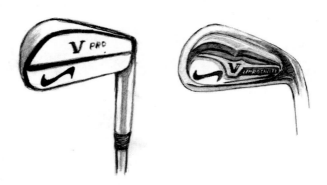

The two basic materials that shafts are most often made of are **graphite** and **steel**.The benefits of graphite as opposed to steel are that the overall weight of the club can be lightened thus allowing an increase in club head speed. The drawbacks of graphite are that it is difficult to control the consistency of the **flex point** (where the shaft bends) and the **torque** (the amount that the club head turns when it contacts a ball). Graphite shafts can also be much more expensive than steel. The cost of a graphite shaft increases as the shaft's playing characteristics come closer and closer to resembling those of a steel shaft. In other words, the more you can make a graphite shaft perform like a steel shaft the more expensive it will be. The faster the club head speed the stiffer the shaft must be in order to maintain control. Shafts come in a variety of flexes. The letters X, S, R, and L with X representing an extra stiff shaft, S representing a stiff shaft, R representing a regular shaft, and L representing a very whippy shaft, usually designates the flexibility or stiffness of the shaft.

There are two types of bags used to carry your clubs. There are bags made for riding in a cart and bags made for those who wish to walk. The picture to the right is that of a cart bag. Cart bags are much larger than walking bags and have plenty of storage space. Touring professionals use these bags because of the large amount of storage they provide. Walking bags like the one pictured below are much lighter than cart bags. Other accessories include a glove for ensuring a firm grip on the club, tees for raising the ball off the ground (on the tee box only),

Cart or Tour Bag

Glove   **Visor** **Hat**   **Tees**

Carry Bag   **Shoes**   **Ball**

shoes to help eliminate slipping, hats to protect you from extended exposure to the sun, and of course balls. Golf balls today are much different from those of the past. They have a variety of covers as well as multiple layers and are designed to travel much farther and stop much quicker on the greens than earlier versions.

It is not recommended that beginners purchase new and expensive equipment. The importance of purchasing equipment that fits you will be discussed in the next chapter. In the beginning it is strongly suggested that you either borrow equipment or purchase equipment that is relatively inexpensive.

Scoring

The number of strokes that it takes you to finish the hole including any misses and/or penalties determines your score on each hole. Your score for the round is simply the total of your strokes for the 18 holes. There are two types of play, **stroke play** and **match play**. In stroke play you simply play and the person with the fewest number of strokes at the end of the round wins. In match play you play by the hole and the person winning the most holes wins the match.

Each hole is assigned a numerical value called **par**. Each golf course consists of holes that have par values of 3, 4, and 5. Par for a hole is determined by factors such as length and difficulty. Par on any hole is simply a standard of excellence we all go by. Par 3 holes range in length from 50 to 265 yards. On a par 3 hole allowing you one tee shot and two putts theoretically determines the par standard of excellence. Holes ranging from 275 to 490 yards in length are usually referred to as Par 4s. On a par 4 hole allowing you one tee shot, an approach to the green shot, and two putts determines the par standard of excellence. The longer holes ranging from 500 to 600+ yards are called par 5s. On par 5 holes allowing you a tee shot, two approach shots, and two putts determines the standard of excellence for par.

Sometimes we make a score that is higher or lower than the par value on a hole. One stroke higher than par on any hole is called a **bogey**. Two strokes over par is a **double bogey**, and three strokes over par is a **triple bogey**. One stroke better than par is called a **birdie**. Two strokes better than par is an **eagle** and three strokes better than par is a **double eagle**. If your scores total higher than the par value you are said to be over par and if your scores total lower than the par value you are said to be under par. Par on most courses is 72 and consists of 18 holes. On most courses, there are normally four par-3 holes, four par-5 holes, and ten par-4 holes.

On the next page is an example of a scorecard. The card provides you with valuable information such as the distance of each hole from the different tee markers, the par value for each hole, the handicap rating for each hole, and the course rating. The card may provide information about local rules, distances from tee markers in the fairway, and out of bounds. It also provides you with spaces to keep your score hole by hole.

HOLES	1	2	3	4	5	6	7	8	9	OUT	10	11	12	13	14	15	16	17	18	IN	TOTAL	HCP	NET
BLUE TEES	454	459	405	366	615	178	384	217	374	3452	376	163	445	537	207	405	567	349	430	3479	6931		
WHITE TEES	447	413	380	350	589	156	372	198	359	3264	366	155	426	527	190	380	490	334	413	3281	6545		
GOLD TEES	424	391	367	325	560	150	364	178	350	3109	360	143	411	497	170	360	471	325	398	3135	6244		
PAR	4	4	4	4	5	3	4	3	4	35	4	3	4	5	3	4	5	4	4	36	71		
HANDICAP HCP	3	5	7	15	1	17	13	9	11		12	18	4	2	16	8	10	14	6				
HANDICAP	15	9	1	3	11	17	7	13	5		4	18	12	8	14	2	16	6	10				
PAR	5	4	4	4	5	3	4			36	4	3	5	5	3	4	5	4	5	38	74		
RED	424	331	345	318	468	105	347	171	318	3827	339	121	401	470	144	340	437	306	378	2936	5763		
SILVER	385	304	330	311	468	105	336	143	291	2673	339	106	378	439	117	334	407	291	378	2789	5462		

USGA Slope and course rating   Blue 135/74.0   White 132/72.6   Gold 126/70.9   Red 141/75.6   Silver 140/73.9

DATE _____   SCORER _____   ATTESTED _____

The Handicap System

Golf has a unique handicap system that allows players of different skill levels to compete against each other on the same playing field. The system takes into consideration the difficulty of the course you play and the scores that you shoot. A handicap is then given to you according to the information gathered. Handicaps are figured in the following way. Take the scores from your last twenty 18-hole rounds and throw out the 10 worst scores then average the remaining 10 scores to come up with an average score. Your handicap will be determined by taking 96% of the difference of your average score minus the course rating. For example, if your average is 88 and the course rating on the course you play is 71.5 it can be said that you average about 16.5 strokes above the course rating per round. If you take that number (16.5) and multiply it by 96% then round it to the nearest whole number the answer will be your handicap. Therefore, your handicap would be15.

Determining your Handicap

88	average score
- 71.5	course rating
= 16.5	average number of strokes over par
x .96	96% of average
= 15.84	or 16 when rounded

When you play against others, your handicap will determine the number of strokes you must give or the number of strokes you will receive. Since each course has its own course rating your handicap will be adjusted for the difficulty of the course you play. For example, a player with a 10 handicap at a course that has a rating of 75.6 would be a more skilled player than one with a 10 handicap at a course that has a rating of 69. The **course rating** tells us the difficulty of the course. The higher the course rating the harder the course will play. The length and the degree of difficulty of the holes determine the course rating at each course. Factors such as hazards, fairway size, thickness of the rough, and severity of the greens are all used to help establish a course rating. Holes on each course are rated as well, with the easiest being the 18th handicap hole and the hardest being the number 1 handicap hole.

When you play a tournament, you will be given a stroke on each of the handicap holes that represent your handicap. If you have a three handicap then you will receive a stroke on the number 1, 2, and 3 handicapped holes on the course. If you are playing against someone with a nine handicap they will be given a stroke on each of the nine most difficult holes. The winner will be the player with the lowest **net score.** To find your net score you take your **gross score** (the score you actually shot) and subtract your handicap. The result is your net score and is the score used to determine the winner. This handicapping system is part of what makes golf such a great game and one that can truly be enjoyed by everyone who wishes to play. **To determine your Net Score simply take your gross score and subtract your handicap**.

NOTES

Name _____   Date_____

Chapter Review

1. What do you call the area in which play must begin on each hole? _____

2. Where on the course can a tee be used to raise your ball above the ground? _____

3. How many clubs are you allowed to carry during a round of golf? _____

4. Which club will hit the ball farther, a 2-iron or a 7-iron?
_____

5. Which club has more loft, a 6-iron or a 9-iron?
_____

6. What two basic materials are shafts constructed from?
_____

7. What is the difference between stroke play and match play? _____

8. One over par is referred to as a _____ and one under par is referred to as a _____.

9. List three bits of information you can get from a scorecard. _____

10. What is the difference between your gross score and your net score? _____

Rules and Etiquette

Rules and Etiquette

The Royal and Ancient Club of St. Andrews introduced the first written rules of golf in the mid 18th century. Those first 13 rules are still the nucleus of the rules used to govern the sport today. As the sport grew so did the need for an overall rules authority. This responsibility was assigned solely to the Royal and Ancient Club of St. Andrews until 1952. The United States Golf Association (USGA) and the (R&A) came together that year to form a unified code. The two organizations meet on a regular basis to constantly improve upon the rules and ensure that the integrity of the game stays intact. The R&A now has well over 125 affiliated countries, associations and unions. It does not impose the rules of golf, but governs by consent so that anyone who wants to play the true game of golf plays by the rules.

The rules of golf are as unique as the game itself. Golf is perhaps the only sport in which the player penalizes himself when a rules infraction occurs. Learning and applying the rules is the responsibility of everyone who plays the game.

This chapter serves as an introduction to the rules of golf. Upon completion you should be familiar with some of the basic rules needed to begin playing the game. A more in-depth study of the rules is advised and can be accomplished by purchasing a USGA rules book and reading it, more than once!

Rules infractions always result in one of three penalties, **one-stroke, two-strokes,** or **disqualification.** There is a simple way to remember which penalty applies to each infraction. If the infraction is due to a **lack of ability** by the player, the penalty is **one-stroke.** An example of a "lack of ability" rules infraction would be when a player hits his or her ball into a water hazard. If the infraction is due to a **lack of knowledge** by the player, the penalty is **two-strokes.** An example of a "lack of knowledge" rules infraction would be when a player breaks a rule such as having more than 14 clubs in his or her bag. And if the infraction **cannot be rectified** due to stated rules the penalty is **disqualification.** An example of a "cannot be rectified" rules infraction would be when a player signs for a score lower than he or she actually made.

Remember that knowing the rules is the responsibility of each player. If you break a rule simply because you did not know it was a rule, it is considered a lack of knowledge and will cost you two-strokes. Below are examples of a few basic rules, all of which carry a two-stroke penalty

You are allowed to carry only up to 14 clubs in your bag during a competitive round of golf.
You may not touch your club to the ground before playing from a hazard or sand trap.
You may not repair spike marks in the line of your putt.

You may not putt with the flagstick in the hole when you are on the green. If you do so and the ball strikes the pin it is a two-stroke penalty.

You may not ask for advice from or give advice to another player other than in areas of common knowledge such as course information.

You must always play your ball in the teeing area when you are on a tee box.

Certain rules are applied more frequently than others. When playing a round of golf the rules most frequently encountered are: out-of-bounds, hazards, lost balls and situations that require a second ball or a provisional ball be played. Whether you are an experienced player or a beginner, these rules is a must. Spend ample time learning the following rules and how they are applied. Buy a USGA rules book and mark each one of the following rules with a highlighter. This will make referring to the rules later easier as well as begin familiarizing you with the rulebook and how it is used.

Hazards

There are two types of water hazards on the golf course, *regular* water hazards and *lateral* water hazards. Regular water hazards are hazards that usually lie between the player and the hole and are always defined by **yellow** stakes or lines.

Yellow line (Regular water hazard)

Lateral hazards are usually hazards that do not lie directly between the player and the hole and are always defined by **red** lines or stakes.

← Red Line

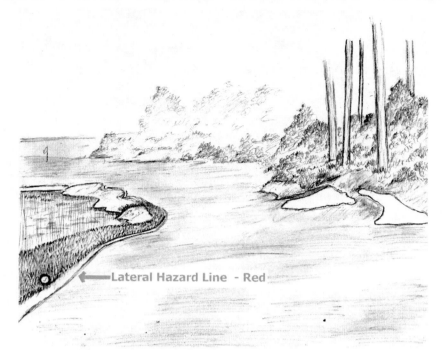

Lateral Hazard Line - Red

There are several options available to you when your ball comes to rest in a water hazard. The options vary according to the type of hazard; therefore it is important to determine if the hazard is a regular hazard or a lateral hazard before you take relief. It is possible for the ball to come to rest within the boundaries of the hazard and not be in the water.

If the ball comes to rest inside the stakes or the line defining the hazard, it is considered to be in the hazard even if it is not in the water.

When playing from a hazard you may **not** ground your club; if you do so it is a two-shot penalty.

When your ball comes to rest in a regular water hazard you have the following options:

> You may play your ball, as it lies, no penalty.
> You may play the ball from the previous spot from which you played and add a penalty stroke.
> You may keep the point at which the ball entered the water between you and the hole and go back as far as you want on that line, then drop and add a penalty stroke.

When your ball comes to rest in a lateral water hazard you have the above options plus the following options:

> You may drop the ball within **two club-lengths**, no nearer the hole, at a spot where your ball last crossed the hazard with a penalty of one stroke.
> You may go to the other side of the hazard, equal distance from the hole, drop and add a penalty of one shot.

Lateral hazards give you the extra two options because it is not always possible to get to the other side, thus eliminating your ability to keep where the ball entered the hazard between you and the hole. On all the above options you must count the stroke that put you in the hazard.

The best way to play from a water hazard is to stay out of them!

Out-of-Bounds

Out-of-bounds is an area on the golf course from which play is prohibited. Out-of-bounds is usually defined by white stakes or a white line painted on the ground but can be defined by fences or roads. **For a ball to be out of bounds the entire ball must be out-of-bounds.** When a white line painted on the ground marks the boundary, the ball is said to be **in bounds** if any part of the ball touches the line.

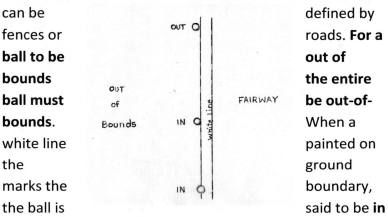

When stakes are used to define the boundary, an imaginary line, extended from the front edge of one stake to the front edge of the next stake, is the line used to determine if the ball is in or out-of-bounds. If any part of the ball touches the line the ball is in bounds.

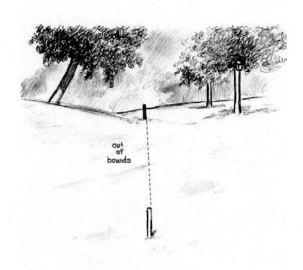

The penalty for hitting a ball out-of-bounds is **stroke and distance**. This means you must return to the previous spot from which you played, play again and add a penalty shot. Remember to count all the strokes including the one that caused the ball to go out-of-bounds. If the ball was on a tee you may re-tee it; if not you must drop it as close as you can to the previous spot.

There are three basic reasons for out-of-bounds to be present on a golf course:

> It keeps golfers off of private property surrounding the course.

> Selling real estate on the course is quite lucrative. This causes course designers to lay out the course in such a way as to have the maximum number of lots available for sale, thus more private property surrounding the course. Most property owners frown on shots being played from their flowerbeds.

> It protects golfers on certain parts of the course from being hit by golf balls.

The shortest distance between two points is a straight line. Holes are sometimes laid out in a way that encourages one to shorten the distance by hitting his ball in a path that endangers others. Out-of-bounds is used to discourage that type of aggressive play.

It encourages golfers to play certain holes the way the holes were designed to be played.

Sometimes courses are laid out in confined areas. For the hole to have adequate length it is necessary to bend it in such a way that makes it vulnerable. To compensate, the risk versus reward factor is only favorable with the presence of out-of-bounds.

Lost Balls

A ball is said to be lost if the ball cannot be found within **five** minutes of when the search begins, or if the player abandons the ball. A lost ball is played the same as a ball that is out-of-bounds; you must return to the previous spot and play another ball as well as add a penalty shot. A player may deem a ball to be lost and play accordingly; however if the original ball is found by anyone before the player plays his next shot, then the ball is not lost and must be played by the player.

Provisional Balls/Second Balls

Many golfers are simply unsure of exactly what a provisional or a second ball actually is much less the proper use of each. For this reason most golfers fear putting another ball in play--and rightfully so since failure to do so properly could result in disqualification. Is it important that golfers know how to play a provisional or second ball? The answer to the above question for anyone who has played golf on a regular basis and has found themselves in one of the following situations is easy: a) standing on a tee box watching a member of the six-some in front of you walking back up a fairway to re-hit his or her tee shot or actually having to make that dreaded walk yourself, or b) finding your ball in a situation in which you feel you are entitled a drop; however, you can get no one in your group to agree, and for a lack of understanding of how to proceed, you simply play on.

If you have found yourself in one of the above situations, you can better understand the need for provisional and second balls. For those who compete regularly, understanding the two is a must. A provisional ball can save time and ease the speed-of-play problems that arise in competition. A second ball gives everyone who is unsure or uneasy about how to precede a simple option. Learn what provisional and second balls are, how they differ, and when and how to use each. This will take away the fear and help you become a more complete golfer.

Rule 27-2: A provisional ball may be played when the original ball is thought to be <u>out-of-bounds</u> or is <u>lost outside a water hazard.</u>

To play a provisional ball, you should:

> Verbally state the intent to play a provisional ball prior to doing so. If the intent is not stated and another ball is played, the second ball played is not eligible to be a provisional ball and becomes the ball in play under penalty of stroke and distance.

Mark the provisional ball in such a way that all members of your group may easily distinguish it from the original ball.

Original Ball

Provisional Ball

Play the provisional ball up to, but not beyond the point where the original ball is thought to be. (If a stroke is played past this point, the original ball is deemed lost and the provisional ball becomes the ball in play under penalty of stroke and distance). If the original ball is found and is "in play", then the provisional ball shall be lifted. If the original ball is not found or is "out of play" the provisional ball becomes the ball in play.

Rule 3-3: A second ball is a ball that is played <u>along with</u> <u>the original ball</u> when one is unsure of his or her rights as to how to proceed.

To play a second ball, you should:

> Verbally state the intent to play a second ball prior to doing so the same as you would with a provisional ball. If the intent is not stated and another ball is played, the second ball played becomes the ball in play under penalty of stroke and distance
>
> Mark the second ball in such a way that all members of your group may easily distinguish it from the original ball the same as you would with a provisional ball.
>
> Play the original ball as it lies. Put the second ball in play from the position you feel as though you should have been allowed to play from.
>
> Finish the hole with both balls, and record both scores.
>
> Mark the spot where the original ball lay so it may be easily found and the situation recreated for the rules committee.
>
> Inform the rules committee of the situation before you sign your card

Never put another ball in play simply for the sake of doing so. Provisional and second balls should be used with respect and only when called for. This is not to say one should fear using them. Simply learn them, learn how and when to use them, and then do so with respect. If you have further questions regarding provisional or second balls, consult your local PGA professional.

Taking a Drop

From time to time you will find yourself in a situation in which you may have to take relief. For example, let's say your ball has come to rest on a cart path. You are entitled free relief and may pick up your ball and drop it within one-clublength of the path no nearer the hole without penalty. Let's say your ball comes to rest in a lateral water hazard. You may take relief within two club-lengths of where the ball entered the hazard no nearer to the hole and there is a penalty of one stroke. When taking relief you are entitled to either a one or two club-length drop. A good way to remember how many club-lengths you are entitled to is by remembering the following; If a **penalty stroke** is involved you receive **two club-lengths**; if **no penalty** is involved you receive **only club-length**.

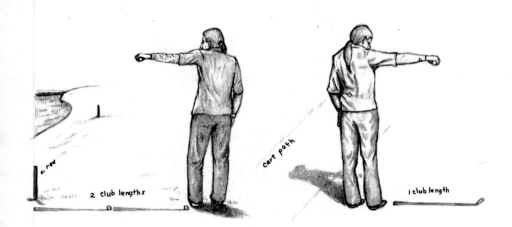

Pace of Play

Although golf is one of the world's most popular sports it's not without its problems. **The most prevalent problem in golf is pace of play**. An 18-hole round of golf should take between 3 ½ to 4 ½ hours to play, depending on if you walk or ride. Unfortunately, weekend rounds can take up to 5 ½ hours or longer. Rushing around the course is certainly not the answer; after all taking time to enjoy your surroundings, breathing the fresh air, and thinking your way around the course is what golf is all about. The excuse is often made that inexperienced players are the main culprits and while being inexperienced does not help matters, it is but one of the problems that affect pace of play. Below are some things you can do to help keep the pace of play up and the game more enjoyable to all that play.

Be at the course at least 30 minutes before your tee time. This will give you ample time to get organized, warm up, and be on the first tee when it's your time to play.

Play from the appropriate tees, tees that match your skill level

Never spend more than five minutes looking for a lost ball. After five minutes you must apply the lost ball rule and proceed.

Never go into water hazards to retrieve balls; once they enter the hazard they are officially property of the golf gods who dwell there. Proceed by applying the rules associated with the type of hazard you're in.

Learn how to play provisional and second balls.

Unless you are in a tournament, play **"ready golf,"** golf in which the honor system is dropped and whoever is ready plays next.

When approaching the green, leave your equipment on the side of the green nearest the next teeing area.

If you are a beginner try to play during non-peak hours

Always wave faster players through and in doing so move completely out of the way.

Taking Care of the Course

Taking care of the course is as important as taking care of you. You're at your best when you feel well and others enjoy you more when you're in that state. A golf course is no different. When the course is in good shape everyone enjoys playing it as well as being challenged by it.

Taking care of the course is the responsibility of every golfer who plays that day.

Etiquette

Etiquette is best defined as the way in which we treat our playing partners, the golf course, and the way we conduct ourselves while playing the game of golf. Below are some examples of good etiquette in terms of taking care of not only the course but also your playing partners and your personal conduct while playing the game.

The Golf Course

1. **Always check in with the pro shop before playing.**
2. Always repair ball marks and divots.
3. Always rake sand traps after you have played from them.
4. Never drag your feet on the green.
5. Never leave trash on the course.
6. Avoid excess traffic around the hole.
7. Always replace the flag after finishing the hole.
8. Never take excessive divots while taking practice swings.
9. Never abuse equipment, yours or that of the golf course.

Playing Partners

1. Always treat your playing partners as you would have them treat you; they are not your opponent; the golf course is.
2. Avoid stepping in the putting line of others.
3. Be quiet when others are playing their shot.
4. Be fair in making rulings for yourself and for others.
5. Be sociable; golf is a gentleman's, as well as a gentlewoman's, game.

Conduct

1. Always dress appropriately; most courses will not allow tank tops or cut offs.
2. Always control your temper.
3. Always play by the rules of golf. If you are involved in a rules infraction be the first to penalize yourself.
4. Keep a good pace; if you're holding someone behind you up let him or her play through.
5. Always be courteous to others you meet on the course regardless of how they treat you.
6. **Set an example for others to follow.**

Safety

Anytime lots of people are together in one place, all carrying a bag full of clubs and trying to hit small round projectiles (that are quite expensive) as far and as straight as they can (in what some might label a feeble attempt in determining the alpha male), only to see those projectiles come to rest in a watery grave some 90 degrees off line, is to say the least somewhat dangerous. Throw in a bad day at work and a not so good haircut and one could find themselves in a "buried lie." Safety is important and should not be taken lightly. It is each player's responsibility to practice safety on the course. Below are a few safety tips you should follow:

If you hit your ball in an errant direction, always shout **FORE**, the universal word for watch out.
If you hear the word **FORE,** always duck and cover your head. Never look to see where the yell came from.
Always wait until the group in front of you is well out of range before you proceed.
Never throw a club while on the course
Stay well behind the person who is next to play.
Never walk onto a tee box until the previous player has stepped off.
Before you take a practice swing always look around to make sure everyone else is a safe distance away.
When holding a club in groups of people always hold it by the club head.
Never walk into another fairway without looking to see if anyone is playing that hole.

Articles & Laws in Playing at Golf.

1. You must Tee your Ball within a Club's length of the Hole.

2. Your Tee must be upon the Ground.

3. You are not to change the Ball which you Strike off the Tee.

4. You are not to remove Stones, Bones or any Break Club, for the sake of playing your Ball, Except upon the fair

& that only

Green ⅄ within a Club's length of your Ball.

5. If your Ball comes among watter, or any wattery filth, you are at liberty to take out your Ball & bringing it behind the hazard and Teeing it, you may play it with any Club and allow your Adversary a Stroke for so getting out your Ball.

6. If your Balls be found any where touching one another, You are to lift the first Ball, till you play the last.

7. At Holling, you are to play your Ball honestly for the Hole, and not to play upon your Adversary's Ball, not lying in your way to the Hole.

8. If you should lose your Ball, by it's being taken up, or any other way, you are to go back to the Spot, where you struck last, & drop another Ball, And allow your adversary a Stroke for the misfortune.

9. No man at Holling his Ball, is to be allowed, to mark his way to the Hole with his Club, or anything else.

10. If a Ball be stopp'd by any Person, Horse, Dog or anything else, The Ball so stop'd must be play'd where it lyes.

11. If you draw your Club in Order to Strike, & proceed so far in the Stroke as to be bringing down your Club; If then, your Club shall break, in any way, it is to be Accounted a Stroke.

12. He whose Ball lyes farthest from the Hole is obliged to play first.

13. Neither Trench, Ditch or Dyke, made for the preservation of the Links, nor the Scholar's Holes, or the Soldier's Lines, Shall be accounted a Hazard; But the Ball is

to be taken out *Teed* λ and play'd with any Iron Club.

John Rattray, Capt

Amendment to the Articles & Laws - 1758

"The 5th, and 13th Articles of the foregoing Laws having occasioned frequent Disputes it is found Convenient That in all time Coming, the Law Shall be, That in no Case Whatever a Ball Shall be Lifted without losing a Stroke Except it is in the Scholars holes When it may be taken out teed and played with any Iron Club without losing a Stroke - And in all other Cases the Ball must be Played where it lyes Except it is at least half Covered with Water or filth When it may, if the Player Chuses be taken out Teed and Played with any Club upon Loosing a Stroke."

Thomas Boswall, Capt

NOTES

Name _____   Date _____

Chapter Review

1. What is the penalty for grounding your club in a hazard? _____ _____

2. How many clubs are you allowed to carry in your bag? _____

3. What color of lines or stakes identifies regular water hazards?

   _____

4. What color of lines or stakes identifies lateral water hazards? _____

5. What option is available to the player in a lateral hazard that is not available to the player in a regular hazard? _____

   _____

6. What color of lines or stakes is used to identify out-of-bounds? _____

7. What is the penalty for hitting a ball out-of-bounds? _____ _____

8. When you are unsure if your ball has come to rest in bounds or out-of-bounds you should play what type of ball? _____

9. What is the difference between a second ball and a provisional ball? _____

10. When taking relief how do you know if it is a one or two club-length drop? _____

    _____

11. What should you do if you hit a shot that is headed in the direction of others? _____

Equipment

The Importance of Club Fitting

In golf, more so than in any other sport, our equipment plays such a huge role in our success. Although a talented golfer can manipulate his swing to accommodate equipment that is not right for him, that manipulation will lead to inconsistency.

Understanding golf equipment today almost requires a college degree. The materials used to build the equipment alone certainly require an extensive study of the periodic table. Terms, like titanium, urethane inserts, inverted cones, tuned weight cartridges, trampoline effect, coefficient of restitution, moment of inertia, center of gravity, and the list goes on, are enough to confuse even a Rhodes Scholar. Every year this technology produces clubs that promise 10 more yards off the tee. In 1990, Tom Purtzer led the tour in driving distance--averaging 279 yards per drive. If you add 10 yards per year due to improved equipment this year's average driving distance for Tom should have been 479 yards. In 2011 Bubba Watson leads the tour in driving distance with an average drive of 315 yards, which is a bit short of that 479 mark.

The truth is one cannot purchase a golf game. The best equipment in the world will not cure a reverse pivot, an early release, or that dreaded chicken wing that has plagued my good friend Dr. Couey for so many years. **Although purchasing good equipment will not by itself help your game, purchasing good equipment that fits you will.**

Most people, upon taking up the game of golf, immediately purchase new equipment. The equipment they buy usually resembles that of their favorite players. It is not uncommon to see a junior who has just taken up the game carrying a 45-inch extra stiff 7-degree Nike driver simply because Tiger Woods plays that club. It is usually not a good idea to have a club in your bag that's taller than you. However using a club designed for Mr. Tiger Woods is a good way to be acquainted with Mr. "Always in the" Woods. **It is extremely important that your equipment fits you and your swing.**

As a beginner you haven't developed fundamentals much less a golf swing and should put purchasing expensive equipment off until you have taken a few lessons and have developed some solid fundamentals.

When you are ready to purchase equipment consult with your local PGA professional, and he or she will be able to guide you in the proper direction. There are many different brands of clubs, balls, putters, and woods available today. Companies like Nike, Wilson, Cleveland, Taylor Made, Callaway, and Titleist are just a few of the manufacturers that make golf equipment. All pro line equipment purchased today is going to be quality equipment. Most manufacturers offer three types of irons, **traditional, game improvement,** and a **combination** of the two. Traditional clubs are usually preferred by the pros and low handicappers because they provide more feel as well as allow the player to work the ball (make it change directions in the air). Game improvement clubs are much more forgiving and are hands down the better choice for 98% of all others who play the game. Combination sets are perfect for those players who need a little help but also posses the skills necessary to work the ball.

The information in this chapter is largely from my good friends at Nike's R&D center known as the "OVEN" in Ft Worth, Texas, and Nikes 360 Fitting Guide. Nike is one of the world leaders in the development and design of equipment that makes club fitting available as well as affordable for golfers of all skill levels.

In this section we will discuss the process of fitting, and what can be accomplished by having a set of clubs custom fit to you. We hope that, after finishing this chapter, you will have a better understanding of the playing characteristics of equipment and how it affects your golf swing.

Your swing is as unique as your fingerprint. Most golfers continually adjust or make swing changes to compensate for poorly fitted equipment. In order to maximize your game, your clubs need to be custom fit to your personal swing and club preference. **No matter how much you practice or how many lessons you take, if your equipment doesn't fit your swing, you're playing with a handicap.**

The Science Behind Fitting

The ultimate goal of club fitting is to create the desired ball flight from tee to green and ensure consistent performance throughout the entire bag. There are six equipment variables to consider in achieving the desired ball flight:

Head design
Shaft length
Shaft flex characteristics
Lie angle
Grip
Golf ball

Let's start by gaining a better understanding of ball flight. Understanding simple ball flight laws will help make you a better student as well as a better player. The two areas that most affect ball flight direction are path and clubface angle. **Path** = direction the club head is traveling through impact in relation to the target line. **Clubface angle** = the direction the clubface is pointed in relation to the path. Below is a chart that will help you understand the effect of the different combinations of the two.

BALL FLIGHT LAWS DIAGRAM

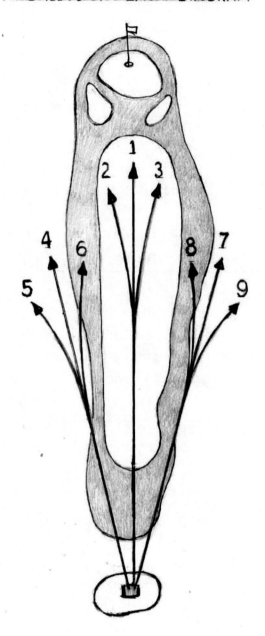

Ball Flight Laws Chart			
	Ball Flight	Path	Club face Angle
1	Straight	Down the line	Square
2	Draw/Hook	Down the line	Closed
3	Fade/Slice	Down the line	Open
4	Pull	Outside - in	Square
5	Pull Draw/Hook	Outside - in	Closed
6	Pull Fade/Slice	Outside - in	Open
7	Push	Inside - out	Square
8	Push Draw/Fade	Inside - out	Closed
9	Push Fade/Slice	Inside - out	Open

There are three factors that determine ball flight; **ball speed, launch angle,** and **golf ball spin**. On the equipment side there are four components that affect ball flight; **loft, club head design, the shaft,** and **the golf ball itself**

BALL FLIGHT INFLUENCE CHART				
	Loft	Head Design	Shaft	Golf Ball
Launch Angle	Primary Influence	Some Influence	Some Influence	Limited Influence
Spin	Some Influence	Some Influence	Primary Influence	High Influence
Ball Speed	Limited Influence	Some Influence [Off center Hits]	Primary Influence [Shaft Length]	Some Influence

74

The shaft is a timing device that delivers the club head to the ball.
The club head and its design apply specific forces to the golf ball.
The golf ball launches according to those forces as well as the attributes built into the ball itself.

The correct combination of the three provides the desired ball flight.

The most important element in club fitting is determining the **correct club head** design for the individual athlete. This is because the club head design has the greatest impact in determining the best possible ball flight. **The primary influencer of ball flight is the head of the club, followed by the golf ball and then golf shaft.** Shafts are meant to repeat impact position as much as possible. The flight characteristics of a golf ball can be influenced much more with head geometry, loft and face angle than they can be with the golf shaft.

There are three basic club head designs: traditional, game improvement, and a combination of the two.

| Traditional | Game improvement | Combination |

The shaft is also very important in the overall effectiveness of the club. The shafts principal role is to deliver the club head to the best possible position at impact with the ball. When fit with the correct shaft, it will load and release at the proper time. The right shaft optimizes launch angle and spin which the club head and golf ball cannot achieve alone. Too often players choose a shaft as well as a certain shaft flex due to ego, pride, and appearance. Short fast swings that produce lower ball speeds but have a large load may require an "X flex" while longer swings that produce very high ball speeds with smaller loads may require an R flex. The stiffness of a shaft is measured as follows; X (extra stiff), S(stiff), and R (regular) **Professionals worry only about results not appearance and certainly not labels**.

The golf ball's primary influence is in providing the correct amount of spin for the proper ball flight as well as optimal distance while maintaining feel. High spin rates yield shorter shots but more control around the greens. Golf ball characteristics are ultimately important depending on club head speed and performance needed around the greens. Tour professionals who swing on average of 110 mph prefer a golf ball with a compression of 80. That enables them to optimally activate the core of the golf ball for optimal distance. An average golfer with a swing speed of 90 mph will not be able to generate enough power to activate a golf ball with a compression of 80. Thus a lower compression golf ball will help them to create more distance. So not every ball a tour player plays is best for the amateur golfer. Dimple patterns will also help determine ball flight. The Nike ONE Tour has a 378-dimple pattern which allows for more shot shaping abilities. The Nike ONE Tour D has a 336-dimple pattern (larger, deeper dimples) which allows for straighter, longer shots. Golf ball will also affect launch angle, but only slightly. Women's golf balls for instance have a very low compression which allows for launch. Players must choose between distance and playability around the greens. **However today's golf ball is narrowing the gap between the two considerably.**

In short the shaft delivers the club head for optimal impact and affects all three elements of launch: ball spin, ball speed, and launch angle. The club head design primarily affects launch angle and has a small effect on ball spin and speed. And the golf ball itself has a very important role in maximizing spin and speed.

Lie Angle and Length

Making sure your clubs have the correct **lie angle** (the angle made between the shaft and the club head) is extremely important if your desire is to hit shots that are directionally consistent. If a golfer has the improper lie angle on his clubs he will more than likely be plagued with directional problems. Clubs with too upright a lie will have a tendency to pull the ball left of the target and will increase the possibility of imparting a hooking spin to the ball. Conversely, clubs with a lie that is too flat will have a tendency to push the ball to the right of the target, and will increase the possibility of imparting a slicing spin to the ball.

Too Flat   Too Upright   Correct

Since the shaft of a club flexes throughout the swing and the arms have a tendency to extend through the impact area, the only true way for the untrained eye to determine the correct lie angle is by using a hitting board and some tape. By placing tape across the sole of the club and hitting balls off a hitting board, you will be able to determine what part of the sole of the club hits the ground. If the tape has contact marks towards the heel, then the lie angle is too upright; if the marks favor the toe then the lie angle is too flat.

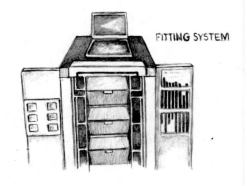

FITTING SYSTEM

The **length** of your club is equally important. If the length is incorrect, the result is off center hits (hits away from the center of the club). Off center hits are responsible for a lack of distance control as well as directional problems. A ball hit off the toe, for example, will travel a shorter distance than a ball hit in the center of the club. To determine the correct length and lie angle most professionals use a fitting system like the one shown to the right. The system is equipped with clubs that vary in length and lie. Clubs can be alternated throughout the fitting session until the correct match is determined for the player. Having clubs that are the correct length and have the correct lie will greatly increase your consistency.

The illustrations below show how face tape can be used during a fitting session to determine off center hits

Too long   Correct   Too short

Shaft Flex and Materials

A golf shaft has three important elements. They are:

1. Shaft flex or stiffness
2. Material and weight
3. Flex point or bend

Ultimately we are always looking for the lightest weight shaft that can provide the most control. This way we can couple distance and accuracy. However, some of the best athletes prefer losing some yardage for more control, so we up the gram weight in the shaft. **The more the overall club weighs, the harder it will be for them to hit it off line**. Jhonattan Vegas plays a shaft in his driver that weights 100grams.

Shaft flex or stiffness is the amount the shaft bends and greatly influences such factors as distance, spin, and direction. Choosing the right flex is important in order to get the most out of your swing. Most amateurs play with clubs that are too stiff. The assumption that men need stiffer club shafts, and that ladies' clubshafts must be very flexable, is usually incorrect. Generally speaking the slower the swing speed the more flexible the shaft must be in order to produce maximum distance. Conversly, the faster the swing speed the stiffer the shaft must be to maintain control. Like most everything in life there is always a trade off; gaining control usually means giving up distance. A shaft that is too stiff tends to cause the ball to have a lower trajectory whereas a shaft that is too flexible tends to elevate the ball higher.

Another contributing factor is the "**kick point**" or the point where the shaft bends during the swing. If the shaft kick point is too high the resulting trajectory will tend to be too low, and if it's too low the resulting trajectory will be too high. High flex points are generally preferred by better players, and lower flex points are for less skilled players. Determining the right kick point for your clubs requires anaylsis from a trained professional. Many feel they can decide simply by using swing speed as an indicator. However, as we mentioned above knowing the swing speed sometimes can be of little value if you don't fully understand the other principles. For example, let's say two individuals have the same swing speed, 100 mph, and it has been determined that they both need a stiff shaft.

Let's say they hit a demo club with a low kick point and a stiff shaft. The more skilled player hits the ball with a normal trajectory while the less skilled player hits the ball in a lower trajectory. The question is what could have caused the difference? The difference comes from the player's rate of acceleration through the ball. Just because they have the same swing speed does not mean they accelerrate the same through impact. For example, suppose both golfers were in separate sports cars and from a dead stop accelerated to 100 mph with the gas pedal all the way to the floor. As the cars pass 90 mph one keeps the pedal down and accelerates at an accelerating rate until reaching 100 mph. The other driver reaches 90 and then backs off of the gas pedal slightly, still accelerating but at a decelerating rate compared to the other. The second golfer is still accelerating but the rate is different. His swing is picking up lesser speed over equal time intervals. Both golfers reach 100 mph during their swing; however, they reach that speed at different times.The true key is where they release their hands. Thus, to correctly determine the proper flex point, both speed and ball trajectory must be taken into consideration.

The weight of a golf shaft and its balance point can definitely affect the flex feel and playing characteristics of a club. The heavier a shaft the stiffer it will play. Again there is a trade off. Heavy shafts play like stiffer shafts; you hit the ball much straighter, but must anticipate a loss of distance. Shafts are made of so many different materials today that it's really hard to keep abreast with the changing knowledge about them. There are basically two types of shafts, **graphite** or **steel**. Graphite can be extremely expensive or very cheap. It is lighter than steel and tends to be inconsistent regarding control. Flexible shafts generally have problems with controlling **torque** (the amount the club face opens or closes when it strikes the ball).

Grip Size, Grip Materials, and Swing Weights

The size of the grip on your club is more than just a little important. An improper grip size can greatly influence a number of factors in the golf swing. The proper grip size should give the golfer a comfortable feeling at address, positive control during the swing, and should not inhibit wrist action as the club head moves into the impact zone.

A grip that is too large can produce the following:

Decreased feel in the fingers.
Inhibited wrist action affecting the release.
Choke down by the player effectively making the club shorter and resulting in a loss of distance due to a lack of club head speed.

A grip that is too small can produce the following:

The club head twisting at impact.
The golfer squeezing too tightly, thus inhibiting proper wrist action
The golfer holding the club too close to the butt of the grip, causing a loss of control at the top of the swing.

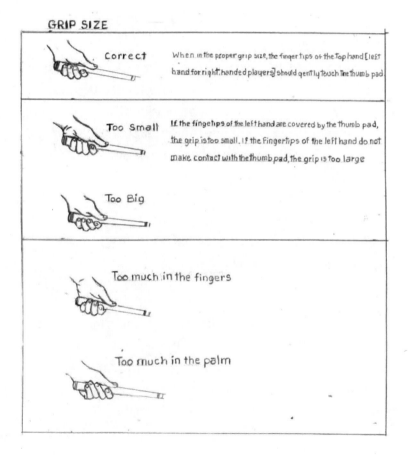

GRIP SIZE

Correct   When in the proper grip size, the finger tips of the Top hand [left hand for right handed players] should gently touch the thumb pad.

Too Small   If the fingertips of the left hand are covered by the thumb pad, the grip is too small. If the fingertips of the left hand do not make contact with the thumb pad, the grip is too large

Too Big

Too much in the fingers

Too much in the palm

Once you have developed a swing and are ready to purchase equipment it is strongly recommended that you have your local PGA professional fit you properly. Since different equipment manufacturers have different specifications for their equipment, it is suggested that you have a professional, who carries the brand of equipment you wish to purchase, do the fitting. As far as choosing a specific brand of equipment the choice is ultimately yours. The equipment must look and feel good to you and not someone else.

Periodically you should have your equipment checked. Extended use can sometimes cause the playing characteristics to change. As you work to further develop your swing, it too will change, and may warrant having your club specifications altered. For example, as your swing progresses and becomes more fluid your club head speed will increase, your hands will be in a better position at impact, and the stiffness as well as the flex point of the shaft may need to be altered to achieve the proper ball flight for your new swing.

Perhaps nothing is more important in golf than confidence. Developing and maintaining confidence is something all golfers struggle with. Confidence starts with knowing that your equipment is the best equipment for you and your game. When the time is right... **"Get Fit"**!

NOTES_____

_____

_____

_____

_____

_____

_____

_____

_____

_____

_____

_____

_____

_____

_____

_____

_____

_____

_____

_____

_____

_____

_____

_____

_____

_____

_____

_____

Name _____   Date _____

Chapter Review

1. What would be the result of having too upright a lie angle? _____

2. What would be the result of having too flat a lie angle? _____

3. What is the most important element in club fitting? _____

4. If your clubs are too long where on the clubface will you tend to hit the ball? _____

5. More spin usually results in _____ tee shots but greater _____ around the greens.

6. What are the three important elements of the golf shaft? _____, _____, _____

7. What is the resulting trajectory of a shaft that is too stiff? _____

8. Why should you periodically have your club's playing characteristics checked? _____

9. What is the trade off for playing a stiffer shaft versus a more flexible one? _____

10. Decreased feel and inhibited wrist action are evidence of a grip being too large or too small? _____

Scorekeeping

SCOREKEEPING

YOU ARE RESPONSIBLE FOR YOUR SCORE!

Coaches, parents, and players spend a lot of time and money in the attempt to learn how to play a better game of golf. Taking lessons on the full swing as well as the short game are definitely important but equally important are the rules of the game, like keeping score. Keeping score correctly is a huge responsibility and should be addressed. This chapter will help you better understand your responsibilities in keeping score as well as how to interact appropriately with fellow competitors while doing so.

The USGA rules of golf have four requirements on keeping score:

> You must have the correct score on each hole
> You must sign your scorecard
> You must have your scorecard signed by the person keeping your score
> You must turn in your scorecard in a timely manner

At the beginning of a round of golf, you will be required to exchange scorecards with one of your fellow competitors. Scorecards will be exchanged in such a way so that no two individuals have each other's scorecard.

At the end of the round, you and your fellow competitors will go over your scorecards and make sure there are no disagreements. Once both players have agreed upon the scores, the cards should be signed by both players and turned in without delay.

If you are playing in a tournament where you have a golf coach, the scorecard should be given to the coach for a second checking before it is given to the scorer's table.

Scorekeeping Tips and Troubleshooting

There are two things you must do when keeping score:

The first is to keep your fellow competitor's score accurately.
The second is to keep your own score accurately.

There are a lot of ways that keeping score can be done effectively and in a timely and respectful manner. Here are some helpful hints:

You should record your fellow competitor's score and your own score after each hole.
The score for each hole should be recorded on the way to the next tee box, NOT ON THE GREEN OF THE HOLE THAT WAS JUST PLAYED! This will slow the pace of play by causing the group behind you to have to wait for you to clear the green.
If there is a scoring dispute, try your best to settle it before play begins on the next hole. If a dispute cannot be settled, look for the nearest rules official, or make a note on the scorecard

and discuss it with a rules official after the round. HANDLE ALL SCORING DISPUTES BEFORE SIGNING YOUR SCORECARDS!

You must keep your fellow competitor's score to the best of your ability regardless if it is a low or high score. You are not responsible for addition but you are responsible for the correct score on each individual hole. IF YOU KNOWINGLY SIGN ANY INCORRECT SCORECARD, YOU CAN BE DISQUALIFIED FROM THE COMPETITION!

Signing a scorecard that has a score on a hole greater than what was actually made will result in the player having to keep that score. **Signing a scorecard that has a score on a hole smaller than what was actually made will result in the player being disqualified.**

You should keep your own score on the designated space on your fellow competitor's scorecard or on a separate scorecard. The scores you keep for yourself should match the scores your fellow competitor has kept.

If any changes are made to the scorecard, the person keeping score must initial each change.

Treat your fellow competitors with respect at all times. Do not turn a scoring dispute into a personal matter.

HOLES	1	2	3	4	5	6	7	8	9	OUT	10	11	12	13	14	15	16	17	18	IN	TOTAL	HCP	NET
BLUE TEES	454	459	405	366	615	178	384	217	374	3452	376	163	445	537	207	405	567	349	430	3479	6931		
WHITE TEES	447	413	380	350	589	156	372	198	359	3264	366	155	426	527	190	380	490	334	413	3281	6545		
GOLD TEES	424	391	367	325	560	150	364	178	350	3109	360	143	411	497	170	360	471	325	398	3135	6244		
PAR	4	4	4	4	5	3	4	3	4	35	4	3	4	5	3	4	5	4	4	36	71		
HANDICAP HCP	3	5	7	15	1	17	13	9	11		12	18	4	2	16	8	10	14	6				
Ⓐ																							
Ⓓ																							
HANDICAP	15	9	1	3	11	17	7	13	5		4	18	12	8	14	2	16	6	10				
PAR	5	4	4	4	5	3	4			36	4	3	5	5	3	4	5	4	5	38	74		
RED	424	331	345	318	468	105	347	171	318	2827	339	121	401	470	144	340	437	306	378	2936	5763		
SILVER	385	304	330	311	468	105	336	143	291	2673	339	106	378	439	117	334	407	291	378	2789	5462		

USGA Slope and course rating   Blue 136/74.0   White 132/72.6   Gold 126/70.9   Red 141/75.6   Silver 140/73.9

DATE   SCORER Ⓒ   ATTESTED Ⓑ

A   player is responsible for the number in this box being correct

B   player must sign the card

C   scorer must sign the card

D   this is where the player should keep his or her own score

Always remember that scoring is a big part of what defines golf as a sport. Each competitor is responsible for keeping a scorecard correctly. Mistakes are made many times that are not intentional by the person keeping score as well as the person being scored so handle disputes in a respectful manner.

NOTES

Name _____   Date _____

Chapter Review

1   Who is responsible for your score? _____

2   The USGA rules of golf have four requirements on
    keeping score, list them._____

    _____

    _____

    _____

3   What are two things you must do when keeping
    score? _____

4   When should scoring disputes be handled?

    _____

5   Signing a scorecard that has a score on a hole
    smaller than what was actually made will result in
    the player being what? _____

6   Who should initial any changes made t the score
    card? _____

7   You should never turn a score card dispute into a
    personal matter. True or False _____

8   When should the score for each hole be recorded?

    _____

9   If there is a scoring dispute, try your best to settle it
    before play begins on the next hole. True or False?

    _____

10 How many signatures should be on a score card?

    _____

The Golf Swing/Instruction

The Golf Swing

Teaching someone to swing a club properly is somewhat difficult to do with pen and paper. Along the way one too many adjectives, a couple of run-on sentences and a misplaced comma can cause what seems so clear to the author to be quite confusing to the reader. **Taking a series of golf lessons is the best investment an individual can make if he or she truly wants to learn to play golf.** Can you imagine where we would be if we had to build our own car given just a manual and the tools? Some of us, a select few would have a car and some of those would have a really nice car. We suspect most of us would have great calves from walking everywhere we went. For this reason we will discuss some basic fundamentals and include a video that will provide you with some visual instruction. It is our recommendation that you seek a PGA golf and teaching professional to personally help you learn the game. For a list of professionals in your area go to www.pga.com.

Getting Started

Hitting a golf ball correctly is about as easy as making a three foot putt on a perfectly flat putting surface—well, it might not be that hard but it's not easy. The golf swing is relatively simple in theory. Swing the club through the ball, keeping the path the club is traveling as it enters the impact area square to the target while keeping the face of the club square to the target as well. Oh yeah, you must also keep the distance between you and the ground the same throughout the swing and at the same time try to generate some club head speed in order to hit the ball a decent distance while maintaining your balance of course. Let's don't forget about the fact that people are watching you, your mind is trying to organize the 435 swing thoughts you're sending it from all the golf tips you've ever read, and the fact that you know you're about to take the $500 driver that you bought because it's guaranteed to hit the ball straight and long and hit a $5 golf ball into a place where you'll never find it in spite of the mad search that will turn up only poison ivy and a hidden chigger farm—nothing to it.

The truth; is, once you develop good fundamentals and learn to put the swing in motion properly, a chain reaction of events can occur and the rest of the swing pretty much takes care of itself—that is if you let it. We will discuss the "if you let it" in more detail in a later chapter. Sometimes learning something as complicated as a golf swing is made far easier if it is learned in stages.

In this chapter we will discuss the fundamentals of the golf swing as well as the role played by the arms, hands, legs, torso, and the club. Once you understand the job of each of these components, putting it all together is much simpler than you think.

Take the time to truly learn the fundamentals described in this chapter. Once you have developed a swing that has good fundamentals you will enjoy countless hours of actually playing the game with a minimal amount of practice required. If you place little emphasis on these fundamentals and only partially learn them, then more than likely you'll spend more time taking lessons and working on the game than you will spend-actually playing it. We've always believed that anything worth doing is worth doing right. As stated earlier in the book, golf is a journey, not a destination. Being a student of the game has been a lifetime occupation for us. In each and every lesson we give we learn something. Practicing and learning the right way are not always easy but they are part of the journey. Challenge yourself and enjoy stepping up to that challenge; be a student of the game and enjoy every stage for each stage has a purpose.

Fundamentals of the Golf Swing

Although there are a number of ways to swing a golf club, some are simply more effective than others. The more complex the golf swing the more difficult it is to repeat. It's been said that golf is not a game of great shots but one of good misses. Keeping the mechanics of the golf swing simple makes it easier to develop a swing that is repetitive. The more repetitive the golf swing the more consistent the misses will be. In order to develop a repetitive golf swing one must first develop good fundamentals. Our experience as PGA teaching professionals, working with several hundred students per year, has been that regardless of the skill level, every swing fault can be linked to a poor fundamental. A good deal of time should be spent mastering the fundamentals outlined in this chapter.

Fundamentals can be broken down into two areas: **pre-swing fundamentals** (fundamentals used in preparing to make a golf swing) and **swing fundamentals** (fundamentals used during the actual swing itself). Of the two, pre-swing fundamentals are of greater importance than swing fundamentals, especially for beginners. A good setup allows one to make swing errors and still hit a good golf shot while a poor setup requires one to make swing errors to hit a good shot.

Pre-swing Fundamentals

GPS or grip, posture, and stance are the three important pre-swing fundamentals that one must master before moving on to the actual swing. Like a GPS system grip, posture, and stance guide us in the direction we must go in order to develop a sound golf swing. The grip is the only contact we have with the club and therefore should be taken seriously. A good grip doesn't necessarily produce a good golf swing; however, a bad grip almost always leads to a bad swing. The proper grip allows the club to remain square throughout the swing, thus reducing the role of the hands in squaring the club at impact. Contrary to what you may have read **it is not the rolling of the hands but the rotation of the body** that squares the club at impact. Do not confuse the near absence of hand action with that of wrist action. Wrist action is important in transferring power from the swing to the ball. The way the hands are placed on the club greatly influences the proper wrist action.

Swing Fundamentals

Once you are able to position the body to the ball correctly it's time to move on to the swing fundamentals. The first swing fundamental that must be learned is the **pivot**. Many refer to the pivot as rotation (the turning of your body around your spine). Without a proper pivot, controlling the swinging motion of the club is virtually impossible. A pivot is defined as movement around a fixed point and that's a good description of what is going to happen in the golf swing.

As opposed to one pivot point, however, we will have two, one for the backswing and the movement of weight from the static address position to the right side, and one for the downswing and the movement of weight back into the left side.

The pivot motion provides three important ingredients in the golf swing:

> (1) A coiling effect where your torso is wound up and loaded like a spring, ready to unwind;
> (2) A transfer of body weight from one side to the other; and
> (3) Consistent tempo or speed.

It is important to learn what your body does in the golf swing before you learn the roles played by your hands, arms, and the club. It has always been easier for us to teach students the proper pivot motion without using a club and especially without using a ball. Learning the proper pivot motion makes it easy to swing the club through the ball as opposed to hitting at the ball with the club. As a fellow instructor once said, "The dog must wag the tail; the tail cannot wag the dog."

The golf swing starts from the address position where the club is basically static. The torso turns around the spine, moving the weight into the right side and then rotates back around the spine, moving weight through the impact area and into the left side in an accelerating fashion. **The rotation of the torso is the power-producing element of the golf swing.** The impression that many have of power stemming from the motion of your hands and arms is a false one. This is not to say that the hands and arms play no role in the golf swing because they do. Power that is generated by the coiling and uncoiling of the torso has to be transferred to the ball through the arms, hands, and the club.

Many believe that you rotate around one pivot point, your head. We personally feel that there are two pivot points, the right hip joint and the left hip joint. Rotating around your right axis point on your back swing and your left axis point on your down swing encourages a turning weight transfer in both directions. It is quite normal, especially during your back swing, for your head to move a little laterally as you turn. A little head movement is desirable; a lot of head movement is not. It is like having a headache; if you take an aspirin it will make you feel better, if you take a bottle of aspirin it will kill you. An incorrect pivot can lead to a number of swing faults, most often what is referred to as a reverse pivot. This occurs when on your back swing your weight does not move around your right axis point but rather hangs on your left side, usually as a result of trying to keep your head still. **For every action there is always an opposite and equal reaction**. As a result, on the down swing the weight moves out of your left side and into your right side, resulting in a multitude of swing errors. The proper pivot motion should have three basic parts. These parts are not separated by a pause; however, discussing them individually makes it is easier to grasp the concept:

(1)   Your back swing or your pivot motion into the right side

(2)   The transition from back swing to down swing as the body changes direction

(3)   Your down swing or pivot motion into the left-side more often referred to simply as the down swing

As you can see there is more information in this simplified version of how to swing a club than one might think. Basically a good grip with good posture and a good setup along with a good rotation and weight shift will allow you to swing a club around your body very efficiently.

Watch the Video!

Short Game
Mechanics & Drills

Putting Drills

The following drills should help you develop your consistency and creativity, as well as increase your feel and confidence.

Developmental Drills

The **inside-to-inside** putting stroke is the most natural way to putt. Developing this type of stroke is easiest to accomplish using a training aid. There are several on the market; however, we recommend  the Putting Plane System from EyeLine. With the Putting Plane System you can feel for the first time a stroke that is "On Plane." It is not a putting arc; it is actually "On Plane." The putting stroke should move back and forth on plane, just like your full swing does. With a 72 degree rail and patented mirror system, you can easily check if your eyes are over the ball, shoulders are lined up, and the putter face is square. Its adjustable rails enable you to practice a perfect back and through stroke that is on plane. The angled rail allows the putter to come slightly inside as it moves back and up and slightly to the inside as it moves through and up. Its light compact design allows you to carry it with you all the time.

The **square-to-square** putting stroke is the more traditional approach to putting. Developing this type of stroke is easiest to accomplish using training aids as well. There are several that can help you accomplish this type of stroke. Place two boards together just slightly wider than your putter blade in line with the hole Distances of three to eight feet work best

when developing the stroke. Make strokes trying to keep the blade perpendicular to the two boards throughout both the backswing and the follow through. Another good drill is to tie a string to a pencil and put the pencil in the ground about two feet behind a hole. Stretch the string through the hole and tie the other end to another pencil about 10 feet from the hole. Make sure the string is about

three inches from the ground. Place the ball under the string about two feet from the pencil. Again practice putting balls from under the string to the hole trying to keep the center of the putter under the string both back and through.

Confidence drill

Drill 1

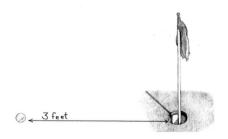

Pick a flat three-foot putt to do this drill. You receive one point for a make and must deduct five points every time you miss. You must follow your routine completely after every putt. The target score begins at 30 points. As that score becomes easy to accomplish, change the target score to 40 and then 50 and so on.

Drill 2

Align eight balls around a hole at a distance of three feet. Make sure the hole is on a slope. This will cause each putt to break slightly differently allowing you to practice short putts that are uphill, downhill, right-to-left, and left-to-right. Try to complete the circle without a miss and again you must follow your routine completely after every putt. See how many times you can complete the circle without a

Feel Drills

Drill 1

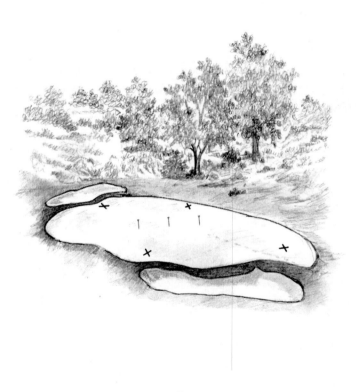

Place three tees about five feet apart in the center of a green that has slope. Putt from each X in the figure above to the three tees trying to leave the ball one foot past each tee. Repeat this several times randomly picking the tee you putt to. This drill is designed to help you develop feel and distance control. Again make sure the area where the tees are is somewhat sloped. This will cause each putt to break slightly differently allowing you to practice putts that are uphill, downhill, right-to-left, and left-to-right. You must follow your routine completely after every putt.

Drill 2

Find a flat 15-foot putt. Place a tee two feet behind the hole on your putting line. Start with 10 balls. For each ball you putt that comes to rest between the hole and the tee you receive zero points. For each that comes to rest short of the hole or past the tee you deduct one point, and for each you make you receive a point. Your goal is simply to finish with a score greater than zero.

Creativity drill

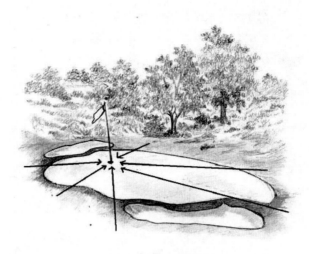

A good drill for developing creativity with your putter is to practice simply putting to one specific hole from many spots **around** the green. Vary the distances from off the green as well as the lie.

Chipping

All too often golfers blame their putting when they fail to get up and down inside of 20 yards. The reality is that 80% of the time they fail to make a quality chip or pitch shot thus placing undo pressure on their putting. Most players walk up to their ball, pick from the bag their favorite club (usually the sand wedge), and simply try to hit the ball into the hole. One problem with this approach is a lack of foresight. The player really has thought very little about where he or she would like the ball to end up if the ball doesn't go into the hole. Another problem is a lack of commitment to the shot itself due to poor visualization as to how the shot will be played.

Golfers who are successful around the greens usually have five things in common. They have **solid mechanics** (which can be taught), and **great feel** (which cannot be taught but must be developed through countless hours of practice). It's been said the more you practice the luckier you become and there is much truth in that statement. They have **the ability to correctly read greens**, and **great imagination skills** such as the ability to play a single shot several different ways and the ability to visualize each way from beginning to end. Last but not least, they understand the importance of **preparation**. They are very seldom faced with a shot they haven't played hundreds of times. ___To be faced with a shot that you've never had simply means you've mistaken the importance of the short game as well as the importance of preparation.___

Every shot requires five basic steps to be played successfully on a regular basis.

1. **Assess the situation**. Take into consideration the lie, the distance between you and the hole, the slope, the speed of the green, the density of the putting surface, and the most favorable place to play the next shot if the ball doesn't go in.

2. Decide which shot is most practical. That is the shot that gives you the best chance to hole the ball and if you miss leaves you where you want to be.

3. Choose a club that makes the shot you've decided on as simple as possible.

4. Visualize the shot you're going to play from beginning to end. Take into consideration things such as the trajectory of the shot, where the ball will land, how it will react when it lands, and how it will enter the hole.

5. Commit to the shot. Play the shot to the spot where you have decided the ball should land and do so aggressively. Expect the ball to do as you have imagined.

To become successful at chipping and pitching requires lots of practice, a consistent routine, and an understanding of the importance of the short game. Without this understanding the commitment to practice and develop a routine simply will not be present.

Chipping Mechanics

As with putting it is difficult to say that there is an exact way to chip. It is safe to say however that the simpler we make the stroke the easier it is to repeat. The two most common problems golfers have with chipping are setup and club selection. Inevitably they stand too far away from the ball, which encourages excessive wrist movement, and they choose a club with too much loft, usually resulting in poor distance control.

The chipping stroke is almost identical to the putting stroke. The biggest difference will be how you set up to the ball. Here are some of the changes you will need to put into place in order to become a more successful chipper:

1. The grip – Since chipping is similar to putting, you may choose to use the same grip you use when you putt. Also, be sure to set your hands slightly in front of the ball at address. The butt of the club should point roughly at the inside of the left thigh for right handed golfers. This will encourage you to keep your hands in front of the ball during the chipping stroke. It will also help you produce a slightly descending blow through impact.

2. Posture and setup. Stand very close to the ball, and get the shaft of the club as vertical as possible. Your toes should be within 8 to 12 inches of a line formed by the ball and your target. This allows you to isolate some of the natural rotation of the body and clubface that occurs as you move farther away from the ball. Place approximately 70 percent of your weight on your left foot at address. This will help you produce a slightly descending blow through the impact area. Hold the club at a more vertical angle than you normally would. The heel of the club should be slightly off the ground at address. This will also encourage you to make a putting stroke instead of trying to overuse your hands and wrists.

3. Ball position. Place the ball on the inside edge of your back foot. This increases your odds of making contact with the ball before the ground thus producing a much crisper more predictable shot.

4. Alignment. Set up to the ball with a slightly open stance. This allows you to see the target line more   effectively and gets your lower body out of the way before you swing the club. The lower body is used only as a support system for the upper bodies 'rotation. Chipping requires little, if any, use of the lower body.

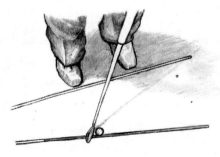

5. The stroke. The chipping stroke is very much like the putting stroke. The speed

back and through should be similar but with a slight increase in speed on the forward stroke. The sensation one should look for is that of the **club**

swinging under its own power and the weight of the club swinging being the force that moves the ball. The length of the backswing and the follow through should be almost equal, with the follow through being slightly longer.

Do's

Always let the lie dictate the shot
Use as little loft as possible
Setup properly
Use no wrists
Remember it is a putt with a club that's not a putter

Don'ts

Try to lift the ball into the air
Vary the speed of the swing back and through
Use more loft than necessary to carry the ball to the green

Chipping Drills

Drill 1

Find a spot roughly three to five feet off the edge of the green. Make sure the area you use is fairly level and the grass is in good condition. You will need all of your clubs and 10 balls for this drill. Start out using the putter and hit all 10 balls. Next, you will use the sand wedge, pitching wedge, 9-iron, and so on all the way through the driver. The purpose of this drill is to improve your feel and to help you learn new shots. You need to become a short game artist, and an artist uses all of his brushes. Repeat this drill from different distances.

Drill 2

Choose a hole on your practice green. Place three tees between where you will hit your practice shots and the hole. Practice using various clubs and flying your shots to the tees in a random order. Your goal should be to use the same method in hitting each shot. You should change clubs, not techniques, to hit the ball to the different tees. This will teach you how to roll control the trajectory of your shots and give you an idea of how far your ball will roll using different trajectories.

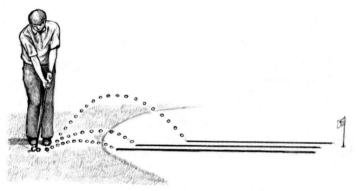

Drill 3

Find a spot a few feet from the edge of the green. Take your grip and stance as if you were going to hit the ball. Leave your right hand on the club and take your left off. Make sure to maintain the angle of your right

wrist at address (right palm facing slightly downward). Point your index finger on your left hand directly on your wrist slightly above your palm. The index finger should be touching the wrist. Practice hitting short chips without letting your right wrist break down through the shot. Feel as if the stroke is being made with the big muscles in your back. This will help you with one of the most important elements of chipping, keeping the right wrist stable throughout the shot. (right-handed golfers).

Drill 4

Place a long thin object in the end of the grip. This object should be roughly two and a half feet in length. You can use a coat hanger for example. Place the club and its extension slightly in front of your torso towards the target. Hit chips without letting the extension hit you in the ribs. This drill is designed to help you with the mechanics of chipping, and will also teach you how to maintain the angle in your right wrist throughout the shot.

Drill5

Find a partner to perform this drill. Pick a spot a few feet off of the edge of the green. Choose one club and a putter for this drill. Player A will chip to all the holes on the green from this spot. Player B will putt the ball in the various holes from wherever Player A has chipped it. Reverse the roles after completing the first trip around the green. Repeat this drill using a different club. Set a goal for your partnership. A specific score or an up and down percentage are some examples of good goals for this drill. This drill will help you learn to hit different shots with the same club, thus strengthening your feel and creativity skills.

Drill 6

Being able to visualize the shot you're about to play is important. This drill is designed to help you become better at doing so. Make yourself a target by attaching three yard sticks together. Choose several areas around the green that will give you the opportunity to hit several different types of shots. Visualize the shot and place the target where you think you need the ball to land in order to roll out to the hole. Land the ball in the target area and see how well you did at placing it in the right place. Repeat the drill using different clubs.

Pitching

The importance of pitching is pretty obvious to anyone who has attempted to play golf. Today's greens are protected by deep bunkers, water hazards, mounds, and whatever else golf architects can throw at us to make the game more challenging--as if it were not challenging enough for most of us. The three rules stated at the first of the book still apply but when you're in a situation where you really have to pitch the ball here is how to do it.

Pitching Mechanics

The mechanics of pitching the ball short distances are very similar to those of chipping. One doesn't use a lot of wrist cock, the set up is very similar (slightly open stance and hands somewhat forward), the legs are quiet, and the weight is slightly front of center. Where pitching begins to differ from chipping is when the shots become longer. More force is  needed to move the ball longer distances especially with lofted clubs. The best way to gain the needed force is to increase the club head speed and the best way to accomplish this is through the use of the wrists. In other words the shot goes from a one-lever stroke, without the wrists, to a two-lever stroke, utilizing the wrists.

It goes without saying that the difficulty of the shot is much higher than that of a chip and thus requires more practice to master.

One-lever stroke   Two-lever stroke

When the shot calls for a short pitch you can use what we like to call a **dead hands pitch**. This is really just a chip with some minor setup changes. First stand taller and move the ball slightly forward in the stance. Next open the clubface slightly and do not press the hands quite as much forward, the way you would when chipping. Finally, make sure you lengthen the back swing as well as the follow through. Allow the arms to simply swing back and through much like that of a pendulum. Remember to keep the grip relaxed and use no wrists. This type of shot actually produces a nice trajectory and the ball will land quite softly.

Dead Hands Pitch

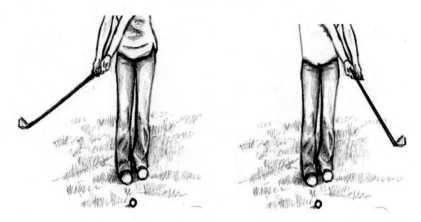

When the shot calls for a longer pitch you will have to start to utilize the wrists. The set up will be basically the same as the shorter pitch. However when pitching the ball longer distances feel begins to play an important role in the shot. Pitch shots using the wrists require a more lengthy swing and place an emphasis on having a nice rhythm. When the speed of the back swing and the follow through vary greatly, it reduces the chances of hitting a quality shot. Deceleration in the downswing usually leads to shots being hit heavy; whereas, a too fast downswing will most likely result in shots being struck thin. The swing must flow. You must learn to feel the weight of the club. When pitching the ball the backswing should also be somewhat more upright than normal. Taking the club back inside or too flat can result in a multitude of bad shots, some too scary to mention.

Tension is perhaps the biggest problem golfer's face when attempting to pitch the ball. Lack of trust is another contributing factor. Tension and fear of a poor outcome, usually result in quick jerky swings and attempts to lift the ball as opposed to smooth flowing swings down and through the shot.

The truth is the drills in this chapter should help get you on the right track to becoming more confident when pitching the ball. It will take some practice and some time to really improve to the level you want, so be patient. **The pitch shot is one of the most complicated shots in golf. This is not due to complex mechanics, but due to the importance of feel and the need for an absence of fear.**

Additional information on pitching:

The more open the face of the club, the higher the ball will travel and the softer it will land.

The more square the clubface is the lower the ball will travel and the more it will roll.

The steeper the swing, the higher the ball will travel and the softer it will land.

The shallower the swing the lower the ball will go and the more it will roll.

Holding the clubface slightly open through the shot will cause the ball to spin more.

Allowing the club face to release or close through the shot will cause the ball to roll out when it lands.

The more the torso is used in a pitch with quiet arms the lower the ball will travel

The more the arms are used in a pitch shot the higher the ball will travel.

Additional considerations when pitching:

The lie determines the loft of the club to be used, a thick lie requires lots of loft where as a thin lie requires less loft.

Check out the landing area for factors such as firmness, slope, and grain before choosing where to land your pitch.

Remember to choose a target, a place where the ball should land to allow it to end up close to the hole.

Think about where you will have to play your next shot from if the ball doesn't end up where you wanted it to be.

Visualize the shot, commit to it, and then play aggressively to your target expecting the shot to be successful.

Do's

Chip whenever possible
Accelerate through the ball
Commit to the shot
Stay relaxed

Don'ts

Decelerate through the shot
Try to help the ball into the air
Pitch from a very poor lie
Hit the shot without being committed to it

Pitching Drills

The Towel Drill

Place three towels at various distances short of the hole. Where you place these towels will be where you are planning to land the different types of pitches you are going to practice. Place at least 15 balls approximately 10 yards off of the edge of the green. Practice landing your pitch shots on the towels you have

laid out on the green. You should notice that the towel you placed closest to the hole requires a higher shot with more backspin and the towel farthest from the hole requires a lower shot with less backspin. This drill should help you develop your feel and creativity along with a better understanding of the different ways you can pitch a ball to a single hole location.

Point at the Line Drill

This drill is designed to help get you in the proper position in your backswing on wedge shots. It is also designed to help you to learn how to impact the ball first and then the ground. You do not need a ball for this drill. First, you need to place a tee in the end of the grip of your wedge. You then need to place a tee where the ball should be and a tee approximately two inches in front of where the ball should be. Next, you need to place a club halfway in between your feet and the ball. Now you are ready to execute this drill.

Make a slight rotation of your chest away from the target, making sure that the tee in the club points directly at the club between your feet and the ball by the time your left arm is parallel to the ground. (See the figure above) Remember, your lower body should remain relatively quiet during this part of the swing. Once you have reached the top of the backswing you should attempt to swing down and hit the first tee about where it meets the ground. This should give you a slight divot and should cause you to break the second tee as well. This will ensure that you are able to enter the ground with your wedge directly at the ball and that you continue to swing down and through the shot.

The Four Quarters Drill

This drill is designed to help you understand what size of swing you will need to hit the ball 25, 50, 75, and 100 yards. You may need more than one club for this drill. Find a target that you can hit at from these four distances. Place 10 balls at each one of

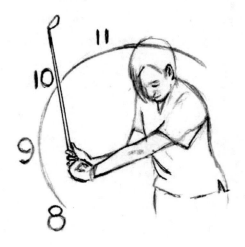

these distances. Visualize a clock around your body and try to get a feel for where you take your hands in hitting shots these different distances. A good starting point is to take the hands back to 8 o'clock and through to 4 o'clock for a 25-yard pitch. Try 9:00 to 3:00 for a 50-yard pitch, 10:00 to 2:00 for 75-yards, and 11:00 to 1:00 for 100 yards. Your goal should be to have a swing that goes to two specific numbers on the clock, one on the backswing and one on the follow through, for each distance. This drill should help you hit your wedges the correct distance more consistently.

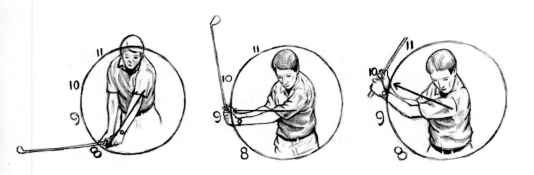

Sand Play

Harvey Penick once said the best way to be successful in playing bunker shots is to hit fairways and greens. Sometimes that is easier said than done.

Most golfers are terrified of bunkers. This is why most players refer to them as sand "traps". The fundamentals of hitting quality sand shots seem to be mysterious to most golfers. They feel helpless in the bunker. That's because the bunker shot is different than any other you will face on the course with the exception of the flop shot. Sand shots are only difficult to play because the average golfer lacks the knowledge necessary to hit them successfully. There are five main rules that golfers must understand when they find themselves in the sand. These rules will help you with bunker shots of 30 yards or less. Once you understand how to proceed in the sand, the next time you hit it in a bunker it will be like a great day on the beach.

Through our own teaching experiences we have found numerous mistakes in the way average players attempt to play their sand shots. We have also observed the best players in the world and have found some things that they all have in common. If you follow these five rules your bunker play should improve dramatically.

Rule #1 Learn the Proper Set-up for Bunker Shots

The first mistake commonly made is that players address the ball with a square club face. One of the most important things that you must do in the sand is OPEN YOUR CLUBFACE. To hit sand shots properly, the flange of the club must strike the sand at  impact. This will allow the club to slide through the sand smoothly without digging. The only way for the flange and the leading edge to strike the sand simultaneously is for the club face to be open. A square club face will encourage the club to dig into the sand through impact. **The amount that the face should be open depends on the distance of the shot**. If it's a short bunker shot the face should be open more than if it's a long bunker shot.

Golfers also fail to align themselves properly in the bunker. Alignment plays an important role in every golf shot and most especially in the bunker. An open stance is crucial in the bunker since the face of the club is open. You must aim left (if you're a right handed player) so that the open face will be pointing at the target.

Rule #2 Understand the Swing Path

The second rule is violated because of a lack of knowledge. Most players attempt to hit a sand shot with a swing path that is very outside to inside. The normal golf swing is somewhat circular in motion. The swing required to hit a bunker shot is for the most part the same. Due to the fact that you're aligning your body open to your target your path is very much outside-in in relationship to the target. In relationship to your body however it is normal. Remember that the face of the club is open as well. By trying to swing even more outside-in with an open club face is a recipe for disaster for most. Keep it simple.

Rule # 3 Learn to Hit the Sand Where You Want

You must follow this rule if you truly wish to become a good bunker player. All good bunker players control two things very well: the place where their club strikes the sand and the depth that their club goes into the sand. Everything else about sand play instruction is based on helping you to be able to do these two things. The drills section of this chapter will have specific practice methods to help you learn these key elements of bunker play.

Rule #4 Swing Through the Ball

The fourth rule is one that is commonly violated. Many amateurs simply swing at the sand or at the ball itself. **In a bunker it is extremely important that you swing through the ball towards the target**. We commonly see golfers try to hit down into the sand two to four inches behind the ball not realizing how much force they would need to be able to move that much sand with such a steep swing. They therefore wind up burying their club head and leaving the ball in the bunker. The other common mistake is that players will attempt to lift the ball out of the bunker. This thought process rarely works. The ball is sitting down on a soft powdery substance. It is important to take some sand with your swing. The amount of sand will vary with the distance required. You must focus on swinging through the sand and the ball, not at them.

Rule #5 Keep Your Lower Body Quiet

The average golfer is much too active with his lower body in the bunker. His feet are usually dancing all over the place and he has very poor balance. When you are in the sand you should pretend that you are standing on ice throughout the swing. Any lower body motion should only be a result of the necessary upper body motion required to hit the shot.

Additional information on sand play

Controlling distance in the sand requires a little bit of knowledge, and a lot of skill. There are a few things that affect the distance that your ball will travel.

The first is how far behind the ball you hit the sand, and the second is how deep your club travels into the sand. The closer you hit to the ball the farther it will travel and the more it will spin. The deeper the club travels into the sand, the shorter the ball will go and the more it will roll.

The amount that your club face is open at address greatly affects the distance the ball will travel. If you open the club face more the ball will go shorter with more backspin, if you square the club face up you will hit the ball farther and have less spin.

Also, swinging the club on a more outside-to-inside path makes the ball go shorter. An inside-to-inside path makes the ball go farther. The last and most obvious effect on the distance a sand shot will travel is the speed at which the club is traveling through impact.

A note about the rules

The average golfer doesn't know any rules in the sand. The last thing we want to see happen to you is for someone to penalize you in the sand. Keep the following rules in mind while in the sand:

You cannot touch the sand with your club at any point before you start your downswing. This includes your backswing. The penalty for this rule is two-strokes.

You cannot test the sand with a rake or your club while your ball is in the bunker. This is a two stroke penalty.

You cannot move loose impediments (anything not manmade that is loose) in the sand. This is a two-stroke penalty.

You can move movable obstructions (anything man made that is easily movable) in the sand.

Drill #1

Draw an arrow in the sand from your ball towards the hole. You will aim your club face at this arrow. Draw another arrow along your toe line that is approximately 45 degrees left of the target. You will align your body along this arrow. Draw one last arrow starting from behind your ball and going on the other side of it  towards the target. This arrow should be parallel to the one on your toe line. You will swing your club along this arrow, back and through. The purpose of this drill is not only to help you align yourself properly to the ball and the target, but also to help you understand your swing path.

For almost all bunker shots, your path is the same as it is for normal shots. It may be outside-to-inside in relationship to your target but it's slightly inside-to-inside in relationship to your alignment.

Drill #2

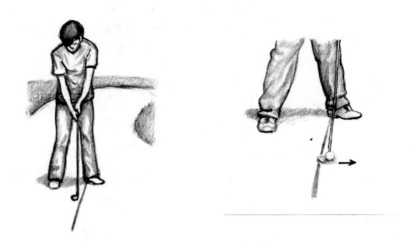

Draw a line in the sand just behind where your ball would be. Practice making swings through the sand with your divot starting at the line and moving forward. Remember when doing this drill to swing through the sand not at it.

Drill #3

Place your ball on a tee in the sand in such a way that you can barely see the head of the tee above the sands surface. Position the ball forward in your stance just off your left heel. Using a slightly wider than normal stance and making a shallow swing, try to simply clip the head off the tee. The closer to the top of the tee you hit the more spin you place on the ball. The lower on the tee you hit the more the ball will roll after it lands on the green. This drill is one of my favorites. It's easier to visualize breaking the tee than it is to visualize hitting a point in the sand behind the ball. Hitting at a point can cause the swing to be too steep resulting in burying the club behind the ball. The tee drill helps encourage one to swing through the sand and the ball. In actual play just imagine there is a tee beneath your ball.

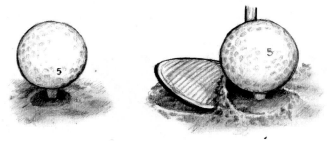

Do's

> Focus on your setup, club face, ball position, and alignment
> Accelerate through the ball
> Commit to the shot
> Stay relaxed

Don'ts

> Decelerate through the shot
> Try to help the ball into the air
> Hit at the golf ball
> Hit the shot without being committed to it

Mental Toughness Games

Games can make practice more fun and in many cases much more productive. We have had many students who have practiced their putting for countless hours on the putting green only to see their putting stats remain the same in events. Making a five foot putt on a practice green is nothing like making a five foot putt during an actual round or is it? The distance is exactly five feet in both cases and the stroke necessary to hole the putt is exactly the same in both cases so what makes it so much more difficult? The answer is simple the one ingredient that's missing is pressure.

We need to practice under the same pressure we play under. This can be accomplished by playing a couple of putting games.

Putting Game 1

[Leave it short or 3-putt... Start over on first hole.]

Set up 9 holes on a putting green from 5 feet to 30 feet. Start at the first hole and try to play all nine holes in succession. The rules are simple;

> If you three-putt you start over (on the first hole no matter where you are)
> If you leave any putt short, even an inch, start over(on the first hole no matter where you are)
> Must finish before you end practice every time you play

Putting Game 2

[Toe Drill]

Set up 9 holes on a putting green from 5 feet to 30 feet. Start at the first hole and try to play all nine holes in succession. The rules are simple:

> You must putt with the toe of your putter
> Same rules as Game 1

The reason these games are so successful is because they cause one to have to think while putting. In an attempt not to leave it short students hit it way past the hole only to find that now they are faced with a long second putt, a miss and .....START OVER.

Game 2 adds more pressure and makes one focus not just on distance and feel like Game 1 but also adds concern about ones stroke. Putts from off the toe can go straight sideways if the stroke is not smooth and precise.

Chipping Game 1

Begin by pairing players up in groups of two. Pick a spot about five feet from the edge of the green and put down some sort of marker. Have one player chip to each hole and the other player putt the ball into the hole. Par is two on every hole. Have the team repeat this to all nine holes and then switch positions. In other words both players have to chip and putt. Set a score for the team according to their skill level. If they tie or beat the set score they are done; if not, they must start over. As the players get the hang of the drill make it harder by adding the rule that if you have to start over you have to drop your target score by one. Start the game having players chip with a 7 iron. The next time the game is played have players use a sand wedge from the same position. This also allows players to start to learn how different clubs react around the green as well as when to use different clubs.

How to Practice Properly

How to Practice Properly

The practice area by definition is a place where you go to practice. The practice area is not a place where you go to repeatedly demonstrate your ability--that place is called the golf course. Too often golfers use the flight of the ball or the result of the shot to determine whether the attempt to execute some mechanical movement was successful. This brings us to Practice Rule #1.

Practice Rule #1

It is possible to make a bad swing, chip, or putt and still get a positive outcome. It is also possible to make a good swing, chip, or putt and have a negative outcome. Most golfers fail to realize this during practice.

During practice, your focus is not always on the target. Many times you are focusing on a specific movement of the body or the club. This, unfortunately, often results in poor shots and less than admirable outcomes. This is where the average golfer gets into trouble. He or she needs to realize that the outcome of the swing is not always a direct indicator of how well you performed whatever mechanical movement you are trying to teach your body to execute.

There is no doubt that how a ball reacts off of the club tells you a lot about what happened in the swing, but this information can be very misleading and almost counterproductive at times. It is possible, for example, to have very poor alignment and still hit the shot at your intended target. Aligning yourself correctly may actually cause you to hit poorer shots in the beginning because you are not use to the changes.   You should not mistake this as a success. While it is possible to have poor alignment and still hit good golf shots, it is neither probable nor preferable.

Change in our golf swings usually doesn't occur as quickly as we might expect. Tiger Woods, who has: the most money, works the hardest, can utilize any teacher he wants, and is an exceptional athlete, took an entire year to fully integrate the changes he made in his golf swing. The point is that Tiger Woods is better than us all at this point and we expect our swings to change overnight while it took the best player in the world a solid year to change his own.

Practice Rule #1 is simply that the result of your shot should not always be the absolute bell wether predictor of whether or not you made a great swing. Remember, it is more important to focus on implementing any needed changes in your technique than it is to have immediate success.

 If you are reading this book, you probably aren't satisfied with the current state of your game. If you are going to make changes, commit to them whole heartedly. This relates to Practice Rule #2.

Practice Rule #2

When visiting the practice area, have a clear idea of what you are working on and what it should feel like. Make sure you understand how to properly perform the drills you are using and they will help you develop quality skill sets. You visited the practice area for a purpose--to get better. Stick to the plan you have developed to accomplish that.

When you practice properly, the focus should be on the mechanics and feel aspects of the swing. To play on the golf course properly, the focus should be on the task at hand--GETTING THE BALL IN THE HOLE IN THE FEWEST NUMBER OF STROKES POSSIBLE. This is in all caps to emphasize the importance of practicing on the practice area and playing on the course.

Some time should be spent on the range practicing not practicing. Golfers should spend a decent amount of time picking out a target, going through their routines, and then attempting to execute the shot. This brings us to Practice Rule #3.

Practice Rule #3

Every practice session should follow a specific method.

WARM UP – FEEL AND DRILLS PRACTICE – PLAYING PRACTICE

Every practice session should allow a little time for warm up, a majority of time for practice, and at least 15 minutes of practicing not practicing, or playing practice. The worst thing you can do is spend an entire session infatuated with the mechanics portion of the swing. This will leave you tight and unable to freely swing on the golf course.

You should spend at least 15 minutes hitting balls in the following manner. Pick a target, select a club, go through your routine, and hit the shot with the expectation that it will come off exactly as you planned. If during this process a mechanical thought enters your mind, back off and start over from scratch. Remember, this is how you will think on the golf course.

Good mechanics are necessary to execute the short game as well as the full swing. The practice area is a great place to work on developing those mechanics. Trusting your practice is a main key to taking the improvements you have made to the golf course. To unleash your short game creativity and instincts, you must have a clear mind. The short game is an art form. Imagine a great painter thinking about the mechanics of his paint brush as he creates a masterpiece on the canvas. This cannot happen. Surely, the painter spent many tireless hours practicing various techniques, but when it comes time to create he must free his mind. You must do the same on the golf course. First you must spend time freeing it in practice. This brings us to Practice Rule#4.

Practice Rule#4

When you are on the course, remember that golf is a game. The purpose of a game is to have fun trying to win it. Leave the practice area behind and it will still be there for you when your round is completed. Golf is a game to be enjoyed and no one has ever perfected it. Treasure your good shots and spend a little extra time savoring them. Forget the bad ones; you can evaluate what went wrong after the round.

What many perceive as practice, just hitting balls and judging whether each was a good or bad shot, does little to improve one's game. Practicing properly, however, always leads to progress and success.

NOTES

Name _____ Date _____

Chapter Review

1. Write out Practice Rule #1 in your own words.

   _____

   _____

   _____

2. What is the ultimate goal of golf as described in Practice Rule # 2?

   _____

   _____

3. What are the three parts of a practice session outlined in Practice Rule # 3?

   _____

   _____

   _____

4. What should you remember about golf when you are on the course?

   _____

   _____

5. Write in your own words what it means to practice properly.

   _____

   _____

   _____

   _____

   _____

Developing a Routine

Routines

Throughout this book certain words appear more often than others. One of those words is CONSISTENCY. Consistency is a main ingredient in developing a quality short game. It's much easier to discuss consistency than it is to actually implement it. The key to developing consistency begins by establishing and following a routine.

Consistency Rule#1

Establish a routine and follow it precisely on every shot.

A **routine** is best described as a procedure that is followed when preparing to execute a given task. This can apply to anything in life, and it directly applies to every shot in golf. The repetitiveness of a routine helps us to carry out the task in a similar manner thus the outcome becomes more predictable or consistent. A good routine can also alleviate some of the performance anxiety that we all feel on the golf course. Consistency can be achieved through a quality routine.

A good routine can also serve as a refuge from the many mental distractions that bombard us on the golf course. Following a routine helps the mind stay positively engaged in the task at hand. A quality routine can help drown out all of the peripheral distractions that can be encountered on the course. It is recommended that a routine be developed and used on every shot during play.

Developing a Routine

Establishing a routine is also easier to discuss than to actually do. Routines can be extremely complex or relatively simple. For example, the routines followed by NASA during a shuttle launch are far more tedious than what you might do every morning to get ready to drive to work. However, both routines are usually effective in achieving the desired goal. We recommend that your routine be somewhere in the middle of simple and complex. A good routine covers three main areas.

PRE-SHOT ANAYLSIS – MENTAL PREPARATION and SET UP – EXECUTION

A good routine begins with pre-shot duties such as analyzing the shot at hand and assessing the conditions of the lie, the landing area, and the elements. This information will help you decide what type of shot you are going to play as well as what club you will use to execute the shot. Neither the type of shot nor the club can be chosen intelligently without first examining these pre-shot items.

Preparing yourself mentally encompasses a few things. Setting up to the ball and the number of practice strokes you use are a big part of that preparation. You should develop a method that positions you to the ball correctly for each shot. You should also find a specific number of practice strokes to ready you for the shot and where you will perform them.

Remember that practice strokes are solely for the purpose of feeling the shot you are about to hit. Incorrectly utilizing practice strokes is a waste of time. Performing these physical aspects will help you clear your mind and focus on the process of hitting the shot and not the significance of it. Last but not least you must visualize the shot you're about to play and fully expect it to come off the way you have planned. Preparing yourself mentally relies upon you performing the physical tasks over and over and over again, until they become instinctual. This is the only way to achieve some form of mental clarity on the golf course.

The execution of the routine is the culmination of all your preparation. Once you have practiced this routine enough, all that is left is to execute it. If you feel bad thoughts creeping into your mind, simply start your routine over. We do not guarantee great golf shots by simply executing this routine, but we guarantee that you will hit the best shots you are capable of at that specific moment. What more can you ask for?

Example

First I determine the type of lie I have; a good lie leaves me many options whereas with a bad lie those options become somewhat limited. This particular lie is good so my next thought is the landing area. This green is somewhat hard and doesn't seem to allow the ball to check thus making a front pin placement difficult to access. The hole is playing downwind which makes the shot more difficult. The front of the green is open and unprotected thus providing the opportunity to land the ball short and run it back to the pin. My yardage is 165 yards to the pin which would suggest a 7-iron. I've decided to run the ball back to the pin so I need my shot to land about 15 yards short of the pin. This means I need to hit a shot approximately 150 yards, with the helping wind my choice would be a smooth 8-iron. I take my 8-iron from my bag and commit to the shot I've chosen. From behind the ball I place my hands on the club and choose an acceptable target line picking a spot a yard or so in front of my ball to help me achieve proper alignment when addressing the ball. (See figure 1) I now visualize the shot I'm about to play and once it is clear in my head I make two practice swings focusing on my rhythm and tempo. I then approach the ball from the side, align myself to my intermediate target, position my feet, and adjust my posture. (See figure 2) After positioning the club behind the ball I take one last look at my target, visualize my shot, and then pull the trigger (See figure 3). I hold my finish position and watch the ball until it comes to rest. This shot is now complete and I start focusing on the next one. This is my routine. Yours may be similar or totally different.

figure 1   figure 2   figure 3

A routine and consistency go hand in hand so its importance should not be underestimated. Developing a solid routine will require practice; thus, the sooner you develop one the sooner you can start perfecting it.

NOTES

Chapter Review

1. Describe and define what a routine is.

   _____

   _____

2. True or False. A good routine can serve as a refuge from mental distractions.

   _____

3. Describe the three phases of a routine.

   _____

   _____

   _____

   _____

4. What should you do if bad thoughts creep into your mind during your routine?

   _____

5. Describe your routine.

   _____

   _____

   _____

   _____

   _____

6. True or False. A good routine requires a lot of practice. _____

Preparing For a Golf Tournament

Preparing For a Golf Tournament

Preparing oneself for a golf tournament is a must. Proper preparation is a cornerstone in building a successful tournament golfer. If I were to ask any golfer how he or she prepares for a golf tournament the answer would undoubtedly be—practice. Although practice is certainly one of the right answers it's not the only answer. Preparing for a golf tournament consists of much more than just practicing. How and what you practice as well as how you prepare other aspects of your game are the real secret. Listed below are some areas that you should address when properly preparing for a tournament:

Prepare your equipment
- o You should check over your equipment at least two days before a tournament. You need to make sure all of your clubs are accounted for and are in good condition. Check your golf bag to make sure you have enough tees, balls, and gloves to complete a round of golf.
- o If you have a yardage book or notes on how to play the course, these should also be included

Prepare yourself for all weather situations
- o Check the weather forecast two days before your tournament. Check your golf bag for proper rain, cold, and wind gear (rain pants, rain jacket, rain gloves, towels, hand warmers, hat, umbrella).
- o REMEMBER, COACHES ARE FORBIDDEN TO GIVE YOU ANY ADDITIONAL GEAR BY SOME JUNIOR GOLF GOVERNING BODIES!

Prepare your body and mind

- o Eating frequent and healthy meals at least 48 hours before a tournament is crucial to your energy levels and your ability to focus.
- o Replenishing lost calories and electrolytes during and after a round of golf is a must. Properly stock your golf bag with enough to eat and drink during the round.
- o Getting enough sleep before a tournament gives your body enough energy to stay focused. A typical golf tournament can last up to seven hours including your warm up time. At least eight hours of sleep is needed starting two nights before the tournament.

Prepare your game

- o Find out what golf course you will be playing for your upcoming tournament. Scorecards and course layouts can be found online for almost any golf course. Once you have identified the type of course you will be playing (e.g. long in length, narrow fairways, fast greens, thick rough, heavily bunkered, etc.) you can make a practice plan for how to prepare for that specific course.
- o Practicing for a golf tournament does not mean changing how you swing a golf club. Even small changes made in the technique of your game should be made at least 72 hours before the tournament begins.
- o Every person should prepare for a golf course differently. You must identify how the strengths of your game can be used to play the course, and how to avoid the parts

of the course that will test the weaknesses of your game.

o Tailor your practice plan to focus on the most used clubs/shots for the tournament course. (E.g. if the course has narrow fairways and is short in length, you should work on getting the ball in play off the tee with clubs other than your driver.)

How to Prepare Yourself on the Day of the Tournament

The previous section of this chapter talked about how to prepare yourself for a tournament before you get there. This section will walk you through how to prepare yourself once you arrive at the tournament.

Plan to get to the golf course no later than one hour before you are scheduled to tee off. This gives you ample time to prepare your game for the tournament.

A golf tournament is not a place to work on your skills, but a place to demonstrate them. You should practice before the tournament. (E.g. you normally hit the ball on a right-to-left ball flight, but you are hitting the ball on a left-to-right ball flight while warming up.) You should play the left-to-right ball flight to the best of your ability instead of trying to fix your swing on the range. We believe the famous saying is "dance with who you brought" The majority of your warm-up time before a tournament should be spent on getting a feel for how the greens react during putting, chipping, and pitching. See short game drills—feel drills.

Any time spent on the driving range should be spent warming your muscles up and getting a feel for what type of ball flight you have for that day.

Being prepared for a golf tournament means your equipment, your body, your mind, and your game are as ready as you can make them for the rounds you're about to play. It means that you know where the hazards are, the speed of the greens, the shots required to be successful at that particular course, and that you have a game plan. It means that mentally you're ready for whatever the course throws at you and that when you turn in your card it will reflect a score that was the best you could do that day. In golf we face only one opponent, the course. That opponent is always up for the challenge. Accepting that challenge requires proper preparation!

NOTES

Name _____   Date _____

Chapter Review

1. How do you prepare your equipment for a golf tournament?

   _____

   _____

2. Why should you prepare for different weather situations?

   _____

   _____

   _____

3. List four ways to prepare your mind and body for a golf tournament.

   _____

   _____

   _____

   _____

4. How do you prepare yourself for the course you will play in your next tournament?

   _____

   _____

   _____

5. Write out three ways to prepare yourself to play on the day of the tournament.

   _____

   _____

   _____

   _____

   _____

How to Play a Practice Round

Playing a practice round

Many students treat practice rounds as an ordinary round of golf complete with a final score. Although keeping score during a practice round is ok it really serves little or no purpose. If the practice round is counted as a qualifying round, then it's not a practice round.

Let's start by discussing the purpose of a practice round and how to prepare for it. Find out what golf course you will be playing for your upcoming tournament. As mentioned before scorecards and course layouts can be found online for almost any golf course. Once you have identified the type of course you will be playing (e.g. long in length, narrow fairways, fast greens, thick rough, heavily bunkered, etc.) you can make a practice plan for how to prepare for that specific course.

The practice round itself should serve as an opportunity for you to familiarize yourself with the course as well as the chance to see how well you prepared. It's a chance to determine first hand

What kinds of shots are going to be required

What areas are troublesome and should be avoided

What pin placements are accessible for aggressive plays and which ones are not

Green speed and undulations

What areas in the fairway lend themselves to making the approach shot easier

where shots can be missed and where they cannot be missed

A practice round gives us the knowledge necessary to plan out how to play the course given our strengths and our weaknesses. It gives us the chance to play from different areas around the green so we can determine speed and how the ball will react from the rough versus the fringe and so forth. We can hit sand shots to see how the shots react from the sand. If you play a course for example that has 200 sand traps and during the practice round you never hit a shot that comes to rest in a bunker, what will you do if you hit 8 bunkers during the round?

Here are a few pointers that will help you prepare for the tournament while you play a practice round.

> While on the tee look to see where the tee markers will be placed during the tournament. The spot will usually be indicated by a line painted on the side of the tee box. Play from that spot during the practice round.
> When playing your shot into the green make note of the distance you have left, what club you hit from the tee, and how well you hit your tee shot. Usually the greens will have a small dot painted where the pins will be placed during the tournament. Find this dot and place a head cover on that spot. Hit shots from around the green to the spot and in doing so determine where the spot is most accessible and where it's not. Mark this in your notes.

While on the green putt from front to back and from side to side to determine slope and speed. Mark this in your notes.

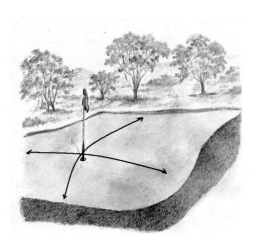

Before leaving the green look back at the fairway
and determine where the best spot is for hitting
your approach shot into that pin placement. Mark
this in your notes.

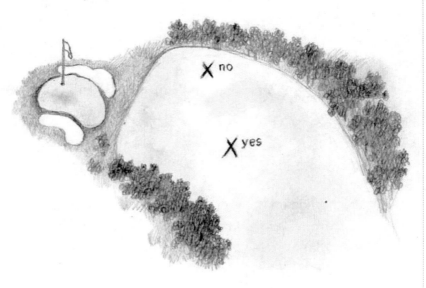

Adjust what you hit from the tee box accordingly.
For example let's say you hit driver off the tee and
left yourself with a shot of 80 yards. Because of the
pin placement your approach shot will have to
carry a deep faced bunker and a shot hit long on
that line will put you in a hazard. By hitting a hybrid
off the tee you are left with a 125 yard shot that
allows you to play at the pin without going over the
bunker or hitting it in the direction of the hazard.
You should hit the hybrid!

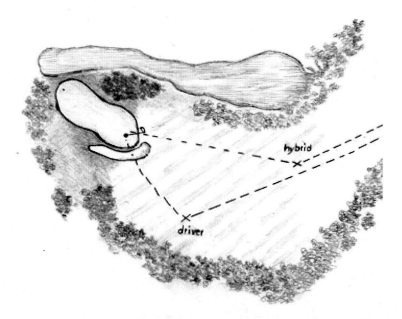

Take advantage of practice rounds. Acquire as much information as you can about the course and its condition. After the round organize your notes and formulate a plan for how you will approach each hole.

Once you decide on a game plan, stay with it. Do not allow things around you that are out of your control to cause you to stray from original intentions. For example the third hole requires a perfect shot with a driver to be in play and doesn't set up well for you with that club. So you determine that your best chance to play the hole is with a fairway wood off the tee. The person you're paired with birdied the first two holes and just ripped a driver on the third. It becomes really easy to abandon the fairway wood and try to match your opponent shot for shot. Remember that a round of golf consists of eighteen holes not three! You have determined your best chance is with the fairway wood so hit the fairway wood.

NOTES

Name _____   Date _____

Chapter Review

1. True or False. It is important to shoot a great score in a practice round.

   _____

2. List three things you should determine by playing a practice round.

   _____

   _____

   _____

3. What is the main purpose of a practice round?

   _____

   _____

4. List two reasons why hitting the driver off of every par-4 and par-5 is not advisable.

   _____

   _____

   _____

5. List the best part of your game and the worst part of your game. Write out a brief strategy for playing a golf course that highlights your strength and avoids your weakness.

   _____

   _____

   _____

   _____

   _____

   _____

   _____

   _____

Playing Competitively

Playing Competitively

Playing competitively at a high level is the goal of every golfer. Some golfers compete against their friends on the weekends. Others compete for their high schools and colleges against other high schools and colleges in tournaments. And a select few have the privilege of playing golf for a living on TV. No matter what level you compete on, your goal is to play to the best of your ability in competition.

Performing well in competition should be as easy as playing well on a Sunday afternoon with your friends; unfortunately, it never seems to work out that way for most golfers. Why is that? Does the ball change? Do you have to use different equipment? What is it that makes competitive golf more difficult than playing for fun? The reason golfers fail to perform as well in competition as they do when playing for fun can be found in reviewing proper practice methods. A failure in competition is a failure to properly practice. Let's examine this problem by looking at what will make you a successful competitive golfer.

Practicing

Most players fail in competition because they have little or no experience performing in competitive situations. This is a direct result of practicing improperly. Practicing should be separated into four areas, with each area having a specific purpose.

Area #1: The Driving Range

You should use the driving range for the following purposes:

> Working on your golf swing through practice drills
> Learning new golf shots
> Calculating the distances you hit your various clubs
> Practicing playing

Working on your golf swing using practice drills is the only way to ensure that you are improving the fundamentals of your golf swing. Hitting golf balls without a purpose is a waste of time. This book has a section totally devoted to swing drills.

Learning new golf shots is a necessary and fun part of becoming a good golfer. Experimenting with your swing and golf clubs to produce different shots should be a part of your practice. This helps you develop feel and gives you an idea of shots you can and can't hit.

Calculating the distance you hit your clubs is very important. You need to know what distance you hit each club. There are two types of distance measures you need to know. The first is carry distance, how far you hit each club in the air. The second is total distance, how far you hit each club including the carry distance and the roll out distance after the ball hits the ground.

Practicing playing is the best way to work on your pre-shot routine and to simulate playing on the golf course. This portion of your practice should include you hitting golf shots at specific targets with different clubs. You should follow your on-course pre-shot routine for every shot. Swing mechanics should be put out of your mind for this portion of your practice.

Area #2: The Short Game Area

You should use the short game area for the following purposes:

> Developing solid short game mechanics through practice drills
> Improving feel through practice drills and games
> Learning new shots and expanding your short game imagination
> Developing a short game philosophy

Developing quality short game mechanics is one of the simplest tasks in learning the game of golf. Using the various short game drills laid out in this book will give you a solid foundation to build a great short game. Without quality short game mechanics, all other aspects of the short game DO NOT MATTER!

Improving your feel is a must for any golfer. Feel cannot be taught, it can only be learned through practice. Use the drills in the book that focus on improving your feel.

Learning new shots in the short game area is a must. Most golfers play the same golf course every day. This leads to golfers developing a false sense of confidence in their ability to hit all the shots you need to play this game. Unfortunately, all golf courses are different. If you do not develop a variety of shots you can hit from the same distance, you will consistently struggle to play well at other golf courses.

To have a great short game you must have a great short game philosophy. There are some basic short game rules that all golfers should live by. Please become familiar with the short game rules listed below.

Short Game Rule 1   Always putt the ball if you can. *A bad putt almost always turns out better than a bad chip or pitch.*

Short Game Rule 2   When putting isn't an option chip the ball but use the least lofted club possible. *Choose a club that has just enough loft to get the ball on the green and rolling towards the hole.*

Short Game Rule 3   Pitch the ball only when you have no other choice. *This is where the pride thing is most dangerous. You almost always have a choice.*

Area #3: The Golf Course

You should use the golf course for the following purposes:

> Playing for a score
> Preparing for the golf course you will play in your next tournament
> Simulating competitive golf

Playing for a score is simply the best means of evaluating whether your practice methods are working. Most golfers fail to play enough golf. **A golfer's skill is measured by what he or she can do on the golf course**. Everything else you do in practice should be based upon improving your future scores on the golf course.

Preparing for the course you will play in your next tournament seems very obvious. Basketball teams' work on offensive and defensive schemes tailored to their next opponent. NFL teams have their practice squads simulate the offenses and defenses of their next opponent. Unfortunately, very few golfers prepare themselves properly for their next golf tournament. This failure to prepare can be traced back to a lack of understanding of who your real opponent is in golf. **Your opponent in golf is the golf course**. Whoever does the best job of beating the golf course usually wins the tournament with the lowest score.

You must do your best to change the golf course you play every day into the golf course you will play in your next tournament.

Simulating competitive golf is the single best way to improve how you play in golf tournaments. This can be done by giving a round of golf some level of importance. Coaches do this through qualifying. Players can do this by setting a goal for the round, or by competing against other players with something on the line. Wagering something as simple as club cleaning or push-ups, can be enough to simulate a golf tournament.

The rules of golf used in a tournament setting must also be replicated when simulating a competitive situation. This is the only way for you to record an accurate score.

Area #4: Your Golfing Mind

You should develop your golfing mind for the following purposes:

> To increase your ability to focus
> To increase your ability to calm yourself
> To increase your ability to stay in the present
> To expect the unexpected

Increasing your ability to focus is important to your success in the practice area as well as in competitive situations. Look to the drills section of this book for drills designed to improve your focusing ability and the length of time you can focus.

One of the reasons golfers fail to perform well in competitive situations is the inability to handle nerves. ALL GOLFERS GET NERVOUS. NERVOUSNESS MEANS THAT YOU CARE ABOUT THE RESULTS OF THE GAME. IF YOU ARE NOT NERVOUS, THEN YOU DO NOT CARE. The key to handling nerves is to first realize that getting nervous is normal, and second, that you must avoid being nervous about being nervous. Welcome nervousness, it will help you focus.

Increasing your ability to stay in the present is the most important mental ability in golf. Staying in the present simply means that you are not concerned with what has happened or what is going to happen. You are totally focused on the task at hand, or in this case, the shot in front of you. YOU CAN'T CHANGE THE PAST, AND YOU DON'T CONTROL THE FUTURE.

Always be prepared for the unexpected. Every golfer gets both good and bad breaks. Handling the good breaks is easy— it's the bad breaks that separate golfers. The way you handle what happens to you on the course has a lot to do with the amount of success you will experience. If getting a bad break catches you by surprise, you are lacking in two important areas:

> You must always be prepared for the unexpected If you're faced with a shot you have never attempted you have failed to understand the importance of practice

Preparing yourself properly through practice is the only way to be successful in competitive golf.

Playing Individually Versus Playing On a Team

When you are playing in a golf tournament with no team format, your concern is only for giving yourself the best chance to win the golf tournament. However, playing golf on a team is quite different.

When you play golf in a team format, you must pay some attention to how your individual actions on the golf course can affect the fate of the whole team. For example, let's say you are competing in the state high school regional competition. Your team has a three-stroke lead on the third place team and the top two teams advance to the state golf tournament. All of your teammates have finished their rounds and you are on the last hole. You are also one stroke behind the first place individual medalist. What do you do? Do you go for broke and have the attitude that if you're second place you might as well be last place? Do you play safe and ensure your team advances to the state competition? These are hard questions to answer. Let's take a look at an example

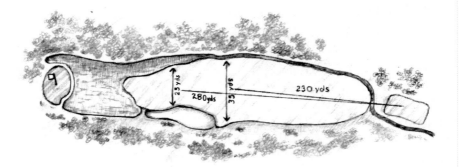

diagram above.

The hole above is a par five of 535 yards. You can reach the green in two shots if you hit a great drive and avoid the out-of-bounds on the left and the water hazard on the right. As you can see, the fairway is 40 yards wide if you hit a tee shot of 230 yards but will require you to lay up on your second shot. A tee shot of 280 yards gives you 25 yards of fairway to work with but allows you a go at the green in two. Take a look at the safe and aggressive paths to play the hole. Which one should you take to benefit the team? To benefit you? **Making a decision is tough but not making one is disastrous.**

Sometimes deciding to lay up when you really feel you could hit that tee shot leads to a lack of commitment and thus a poor layup. Only you know what feels right at that moment. If you have prepared properly you'll have a gut feeling and you should always trust in yourself and that feeling. Playing well in competition is the ultimate goal of any golfer.

Use this chapter to craft an effective practice method for the driving range, the short game area, the golf course, and improving your mental skills. The more you prepare the more competitive you will be.

NOTES

Name _____ Date _____

Chapter Review

1. List three factors that make playing golf competitively different than playing golf for fun.

   _____

   _____

   _____

2. How should a player utilize his or her time on the driving range to prepare for competitive golf?

   _____

   _____

   _____

3. What are the four areas of your short game you should work on when preparing to play competitively?

   _____

   _____

   _____

   _____

4. What is the most important method used to evaluate whether your practice methods are working?

   _____

5. What is the most important mental ability in golf?

   _____

6. Define staying in the present.

   _____

   _____

   _____

Mental Aspects of the Game

What you think about you bring about!

Many different ingredients are needed to become a successful golfer. In the latter chapters of this book we have discussed the importance of developing a routine, preparing for a tournament, how to play a practice round, and playing competitively. We have discussed the importance of getting fit with the proper equipment. All the pieces are in place with the exception of one. A friend of Ray's, Dr. David Cook, once made a statement that he felt was so profoundly important he based every aspect of his teachings around it. "**Every voluntary muscle movement begins with a thought.**" "That statement opened my eyes to perhaps the single most important fundamental in golf, and yet I had never even given it a thought. Dr. Cook followed that statement with one that has had even a greater impact on my teachings, **"we have the ability to control that thought".**"

The argument has always been made that golf is more physical in the beginning and becomes more mental as you advance. The truth is from the very beginning, the first time you pick up a club, golf is 100% mental. **The mindset that we have in learning is as important as the mindset we have in performing**. As Dr. Cook said, we can control that, and controlling it is something we must do from the beginning. Controlling the way you think can greatly increase the rate at which you learn, as well provide the foundation necessary to become a successful player. To understate the importance of becoming **mentally fit** would be a rules infraction punishable by a lifetime of frustration playing a game that should provide a lifetime of fulfillment.

Tommy Bolt once said "the mind messes up more shots than the body." Tour players have always been aware of the mental aspects of the game but only a few ever came to understand and accept them. None come to mind more than Jack Nicklaus and Tiger Woods. Tom Layman, a PGA touring professional and winner of two majors, when asked of all the players on the tour that he feared most replied "myself." I think if asked the same question both Jack and Tiger would reply "no one." Tiger and Jack are great players because of their sound mindset and not in spite of it. **The most influential message you'll ever receive in life comes from yourself.**

Mental Aspects of Learning

The following is an overview of Dr. Cook's approach to the mental aspects of learning and the game. For more information about Dr. Cook and his work please visit **www.mindsetacademy.com**.

Choose to believe in your method – Find *your* swing, not *the* swing.

> Be a student of your game
> Know why you do what you do
> Seek to understand your swing, and then spend your life developing it.
> Establish your foundations
> Don't play a round without them.

Choose positive inner coaching – "To be a great player, you have to be a great coach ... to yourself"

Our mind communicates to our muscles through words and images.

Every voluntary muscle movement begins with a thought.

... Therefore, the origin of every golf swing is in the mind.

Choose your words carefully; they control the shot.

You have to take control of your thoughts; be pro-active, know what you are going to think ahead of time.

The most influential message you'll ever receive in life comes from yourself.

Choose to visualize success – "Every shot starts with an empty canvas; it is your task to paint a Picasso. (Johnny Arreaga)

Images are inevitable: Do you choose to see success or failure?

Seeing the shot sets the "wheels in motion" for the actual shot.

Visualizing the shot is a pre-requisite for feeling the shot (i.e. timing, tempo, rhythm)

Learning takes place when you mentally create the shot.

At the very least, visualizing is becoming target oriented.

Choose to see three things as vividly as possible when visualizing:

1. Aiming point
2. Shape of shot
3. Trajectory

Choose to trust your instincts – "Trust is simply the courage to let go and let it happen."

- Trust is letting go of mechanical control. Once you learn to dance you don't count the steps.
- Trust releases instincts; doubt locks them inside.
- Trust is earned by first seeing, then feeling the shot to be made
- The errors of trust include:
    1. Pressing – increasing the importance of a given shot
    2. Guiding – playing away from trouble rather than to a target
    3. Over aiming – the target becomes too specific, creates tension
    4. Jamming – the mind has too many mechanical thoughts or commands

Choose mental toughness – "Loving to test yourself in the heat of the battle is the seed of a competitive spirit. Consistently putting yourself on the line in competition produces mental toughness.

> Mental toughness is the ability to handle adversity in "the heat of competition" with positive inner coaching.
> Mental toughness is a learned skill
> Preparing a response ahead of time is the key to responding in the heat of battle.
> We must be prepared for the "realities" of golf.
> Every shot won't go where we plan for it to go.
> See golf's obstacles as challenges rather than setbacks.

It is hard to "block out" distractions, but it is relatively simple to replace them.

Choose a pre-shot mindset – "Your number one goal in golf must be to put your mind in position to score over every shot."

Taking control of the conscious mind puts you in control of your performance.
Golf is as much a game of overcoming the distractions as it is swinging well.
Concentration is the focus of attention

There are four distinct phases of concentration, which must be used over every shot.
1. Broad External (observe all the variables)
2. Broad Internal (develop a strategy)
3. Narrow External (choose a target)
4. Narrow Internal (focus on one thought as the swing starts)

Developing a pre shot mindset is the foundation for consistent concentration.
1. The decision phase
   A. **Observe**: layout, elevation change, yardage, wind, lie, hazards break, grain...

   B. **Strategy**: choose target, type of shot, and club.

2. Shot making phase

   A. "**See it**" paint the shot; see success.

   B. "**Feel it**" feel the swing needed to produce the visualized shot

C. **"Trust it"** this triggers club head movement and the giving up of mechanical control

Choose an effective perspective – "There are no *crucial shots* in the game of golf."

Golf is a game, not brain surgery
Your self-worth has nothing to do with the score you post.
Put your mind in position to score over each shot, then take a "walk in the park" between shots.
Golf is a privilege; enjoy it.
Have fun
A bad day on the golf course is still better than a good day figuring taxes.

How to Practice

To improve one has to practice. Developing good fundamentals both mentally and physically requires not just practice, but proper practice. For a practice session to be successful two ingredients must be present; the proper mindset and a clear picture of what is to be accomplished during the session.

Simply hitting balls into the range as fast as you can with different clubs will not help you improve your swing, although it may help you become more aerobically fit.

Have a plan when you're practicing both mentally and physically. Entering the practice session with the proper mindset almost always ensures you of a successful session. Be positive; the learning process is part of the game— enjoy it.

Have a clear picture of what you're trying to accomplish, how you're going to accomplish it, and how you are going to measure the success of the session. Too often golfers rate a practice session on how well they hit the ball. Working on drills to develop proper mechanics does not always produce good shots. To strike the ball properly requires the mind to be free of mechanical thoughts.

There are basically two types of practice sessions. They are practice sessions designed to help you develop better fundamentals, and practice sessions designed to help you free your mind and play the game. When practicing fundamentals mechanics are important and should be the focus of the session. Success is based on the feel you developed during the session, not where the ball goes. Practice sessions designed to free your mind are free of mechanics. The focus is on the routine and the thought process and the ball flight, not mechanics.

Having a routine is important in that it helps to occupy the mind in a positive way. The thought process and ball flight are extremely important. If you cannot develop a clear picture of what you want the ball to do, you will have minimal success. It's difficult to accomplish what you cannot see yourself accomplishing. Mental imagery helps clear the mind of mechanics and gives the brain a good clear picture of the task at hand. Although many may disagree the mental practice is far more rewarding than the mechanical one.

Things that are difficult are only difficult because we choose to see them in that manner. Success is something everyone can experience by simply allowing it to happen. When a student tells us that he or she was scared to hit a specific shot we can't help but wonder what they are afraid of. There is no place for fear in golf—it is a game. Fear causes tension and tension ruins any hopes of having a successful repetitive golf swing. **When faced with a difficult shot one should be excited about the challenge, not afraid of the outcome.**

Learning occurs in four stages. First, you have no idea that you have no idea. This stage is where we all start. It looks simple enough and if he or she can do it, I'm sure that I can. After being frustrated for some time, you reach stage two; you have a very good idea that you had no idea. This is where you come to the conclusion that there is more to it than meets the eye and acknowledge that help is needed.

Next is stage three; you know that you know. In other words you have the knowledge and the skills to accomplish the feat. Finally, comes stage four, you must forget you know and simply do. Most never reach stage four, but choose instead to exist in stage three. Walking is as complicated a movement as the golf swing. Think back to the last lesson you received on how to walk. Once you got the mechanics down, you simply forgot them and began a lifetime of walking successfully, without weekly lessons. Some might say that this is a poor example, that walking is simple, and could be done blindfolded. If you asked those who feel this way to try to walk on a six inch wide board lying on the ground for a distance of thirty feet, their reply would be—no problem. If that board were placed between two buildings some ninty stories tall, their reply would be—no way.

The point is that walking is walking no matter where you do it. It only becomes difficult when the thought of failure enters the brain. Be positive, enjoy the learning process and then simply play.

Competitive Golf

Playing the Game

The mental rules of the game:

1. Always have a procedure to a specific target
2. Play each shot one shot at a time to the best of your ability at that moment
3. When the shot does not please you, forgive and forget, then play the next shot to the best of your ability, at that moment
4. Continue this procedure until all 18 holes are played
5. Post the score
6. After the round, applaud your best efforts, then analyze your mistakes, correct them in your mind, and the round is finished
7. Compare yourself to no one else—only the golfer you know you can be
8. Respect the procedure and post a new score, letting yourself get closer to the edge of your ability

Things to remember

1. In golf as in life, the attempt to do something in one stroke that needs two strokes is apt to result in taking three.
2. Once you learn to strike the ball, course management and psychology become the dominant factors in successfully playing the game. If you can't manage yourself and the course, you can't play.
3. Golf is a compromise of what your ego wants you to do, what experience tells you to do, and what your nerves will let you do.

4. Competitive golf is played on a 5 $^1/_2$ inch course, the space between your ears.
5. Golf is not a game of great shots but one of the most accurate misses. The people who make the smallest mistake win.

Rules for Focus

1. You and only you are responsible for your score, good or bad.
2. Never work on mechanics during a round of golf.
3. At the advanced level the most important aspect of your game is your mental attitude. You must develop a mindset that allows you to be able to concentrate on the task at hand, playing each hole to the best of your ability.
4. In order to accomplish rule 3 you must rid yourself of all feelings that interrupt concentration such as

Pride
Fear
Doubt
Hope/Luck

Pride and fear destroy one's ability to think logically. Never be so proud that you play a shot you know is not logical. Golf is a game, and regardless of the outcome life goes on. There is nothing to fear. Never doubt in your ability; trust in yourself and your skills. **THERE IS NO ROOM FOR**

LUCK. When you attempt a shot it is not that you hope it will work, but that you know it will work, because you have done it enough to trust its outcome.

To play golf and be able to score under pressure you must have:

A simple and easy swing

Confidence in your short game

No fear of obstacles

For example, do not hit an iron just because a fairway has bunkers. Learn to play out of them and the fairway will suddenly appear very wide and your swing will feel freer.

Know your Game

Your Strengths
Your weakness

What you cannot do in practice you probably cannot do in competition. You are not playing those that you may be paired with. You are playing the golf course.

Paradoxes of Golf

To play better, think less.

To hit it farther, swing easier.

To gain control, give up control.

A hard shot requires a soft touch.

Adding emotions lessens potential.

When hitting a difficult shot, you play aggressively to a conservative target.

Short shots cause the highest pressure.

The goal is simple in golf; the paths are many.

There is only one target, but many distractions.

Great swings don't always produce great shots.

Many times the harder you try the worse it gets.

Golf is very technical, but must be played very simply.

The Mental Aspects of Playing

See the fairway not the water. When a negative thought enters your mind replace it with a positive one. This advice is easy to give, but hard to follow. Regardless of what you do you will see the water, and whether you like it or not from time to time negative thoughts will enter your mind. Being prepared is all you can do. Know that each time you play you will be faced with challenges. When they arrive embrace them. If you were perfect the game would be boring. Challenges are why we play in the first place. If a negative thought comes to mind ignore it. Replacing it with a positive one means you just entered into a dialogue with yourself. I'm not sure but I don't think that's healthy and is perhaps illegal in several states. The only reason that thought exists is because you chose to allow it. Fear of failure is not something we are born with; it's something we learn. Juniors have possessed all the best putting strokes I've ever witnessed. I had an eight year old in my academy who once made 374 three footers without missing for a 75-cent coke. When you tell a four-year-old you'll buy him his favorite toy if he can hit a ball 150 yards in the air, he will spend hours trying to accomplish a feat that we know is impossible. It never crosses his mind that he might not be able to do it. Along the way we lose that "I can do anything attitude" and regardless of how hard we try, we never regain it.

As we grow older we are taught to think logically, be realistic, and to overanalyze ourselves. We judge our every move and place a great deal of emphasis on not making mistakes. **Mistakes are a part of life; if you haven't made one then you've never applied yourself.**

"I missed more than 9,000 shots in my career. I've lost almost 300 games. Twenty-six times I've been trusted to take the game-winning shot and missed. I have failed over and over again in my life. And that is why I succeed." Michael Jordan 1998

Perhaps the idea that we can accomplish anything is childish. If so, my advice is to play the game like a child. Be excited by the challenges put before you and eager to show off your skills. Believe that all is possible and—Just Play.

Attitude

"The longer I live, the more I realize the impact of attitude on life. Attitude, to me, is more important than facts. It is more important than the past, than education, than money, than circumstances, than failures, than successes, than what other people think or say or do. It is more important than appearance, giftedness or skill. It will make or break a company...a church...a home. The remarkable thing is that we have a choice everyday regarding the attitude we will embrace for that day. We cannot change our past.... we cannot change the fact that people will act in a certain way. We cannot change the inevitable. The only thing we can do is play on the one string we have, and that is our attitude.... I am convinced that life is 10% what happens to me and 90% how I react to it."

NOTES

Preparing for College Recruiting

The 411 on College Recruitment

Understanding the recruiting process and the NCAA Recruiting Rules can be especially helpful to a junior golfer hoping to play college golf at any level. Numerous resources are available to help you get started on the process, including the National Collegiate Athletic Association (NCAA) Eligibility Center (often called and previously called the NCAA Clearing house). http://eligibilitycenter.org You can also visit www.ncaa.org and find out more about the student-athlete experience.

It is really never too early to begin the process of preparing yourself for recruitment and a clear idea of how things work can be extremely beneficial. Learning from others who have gone through the process could be helpful, but be very careful of friends, who tell you "the rules", because there's a good chance, that while they have good intentions, they may not be accurate.

Generally speaking, in ninth grade a junior golfer would become a Prospective Student-Athlete (PSA) for recruiting purposes.
Although it is not necessary at this stage, sometime before the junior year of high school it is important to register with the NCAA Eligibility Center and complete all the necessary documentation so there would be no hang-ups in recruitment.
Athletically there are items to note, like amateurism status, but equally important are the academic requirements including core classes and college entrance tests like the SAT or ACT. Check with your school counselor to make sure you are enrolled in classes that meet the NCAA's criteria.

Do your homework:

Decide what schools in which you may be interested and begin learning about the academic standards at the institution(s) and the standards for the caliber of golf necessary to be a part of those programs.

Be realistic about the level of your game, but don't short change yourself or not dare to dream big.

A PSA can begin calling coaches, emailing schools, and making unofficial visits to schools at any age (usually beginning in 9th and 10th grades), however, be aware, that schools and coaches cannot call or have face to face contact with you until much later. You can learn more about what can and can't happen related to these matters by visiting the NCAA website.

In brief—an unofficial visit is one where the PSA bears the expense. There is no limit on how many of these can occur and where they can occur, including more than one to the same place.

An official visit is one where a school is allowed to bear the expense for the visit insofar as rules allow.

In tenth grade—take the pre-college entrance tests offered, like the PSAT and PACT.

In eleventh grade, begin taking the college entrance exams and recognize there is no limit on the number of times a PSA may sit for the exams. The NCAA rules allow a PSA to take the best scores from the tests to gain the best aggregate score to use.

You could use your verbal score from one test and your math score from another to get your best total.
You will need to begin to make sure your high school transcript and appropriate information is sent to the NCAA Eligibility Center.

Beginning on September 1st of the PSA's junior year in high school, college coaches may write and/or email PSA's. College coaches may not call a PSA until July 1st following the PSA's junior year in high school, and even then the number of calls is limited to 1 per week. Coaches are not allowed to text a PSA at anytime. Coaches are limited to three contacts (face-to-face encounters not part of an unofficial or official visit). Coaches are limited to four evaluations of a PSA (which may or may not include a contact). Basically, a college coach could say "hello" to you and it not count as a contact, but anything that goes beyond a casual greeting is considered a contact and if a PSA isn't of age, it could be a violation of NCAA rules.

During a PSA's senior year of high school, up to five official visits may be made to schools (no more than one visit to each school). An official visit is a 48-hour visit to a school with very specific rules concerning what is an allowable activity for the school and the PSA.

PSA's who are extended opportunities for scholarships at schools will sign a National Letter of Intent, or a similar document depending on the school, during one of two official signing periods, November (early signing period) or April of their senior years.

There are many thoughts on how to become noticed by college coaches. The short answer to the challenge is: play well and you will get noticed. It isn't always that easy, though. Making sure coaches have received your resume with current email, home address, phone numbers, coaches names and numbers, professional swing instructor's names and numbers, and even a swing video on a DVD or thumb drive is very helpful. Set up a very specific email address just for recruiting such as (YOUR FIRST NAME.LAST NAME) @ gmail.com. This makes it much easier for coaches to remember you as opposed to a nick name. You want to separate yourself from all the other candidates and coaches love to put a face with a name, so be sure to include a picture. Make the letter personable and professional. No coach wants a mass mailer any more than you want one from a coach or school. If you don't know the coach's name, jump on the internet and find it.

Find the very best competition you can and play against it. Certainly national junior golf tours exist and receive a lot of attention from college coaches. Many regional junior tours do as well. Some players can afford them and some cannot. Regardless find the best competition you can and play against it. This exposes you to pressure and gets you on the largest stages possible. Playing a high school event at some 4,800 yards for girls when college tournaments are 6,200 yards is a big difference. Play USGA qualifying events. Play state, regional, or national amateur events or qualifiers.

Coaches certainly want a fundamentally sound golf swing from those they recruit, but they truly want golfers who can play the game! You have to post a score. Do you know how to golf your ball? Can you manage yourself, your emotions, the course, your school work, and your parents? Coaches want a golf swing, but they want a golfer more.

Think of questions you want to ask potential coaches about how they manage their team, their team's schedule, and the expectations of you as a player and a student-athlete.

⦿ What size squad do you want to have? How many players do you expect to sign in the next couple of years?
⦿ Is there scholarship money available to someone at my level? What is the range of that? What expectations must be met in order to see that amount increase? Is it possible for it to increase? What might cause it to decrease?
⦿ How are practices structured?
⦿ What is the conditioning schedule and off-season schedule?
⦿ Are study hall hours and/or tutorial hours required? If so, how many, and when?
⦿ How do you determine who will play in tournaments? What does qualifying look like?
⦿ What is your coaching style? What type players generally succeed in your program?

In addition be prepared to offer answers to the questions below, and perhaps volunteer some of this information in the course of conversation to prevent being asked and show you realize what things coaches want to know.

What are your goals for college golf and academics?
Why "our" school and program?
What are your scholarship expectations and/or needs?
Assess the strengths and weaknesses of your golf game

What are the main items you will consider when making your final decisions about where to attend college and play golf?

When are you planning to make your final decision/sign?

Describe an ideal practice session for yourself.

What is your upcoming tournament schedule?

Have you registered with the NCAA Eligibility Center? Registered for or taken the SAT/ACT exams?

Prepare for the time you will spend talking to coaches by practicing the answers to these questions. They shouldn't sound rehearsed, but they also shouldn't sound like you've never thought about the answers to these questions before. Also practice answering the questions and NOT having your parents answer them. A parent answering for the student-athlete can send up major red-flags to a potential coach.

If possible, have a swing DVD and/or resume with you when you meet with a coach if they don't have one from you already.

Keep the video simple and include shots from side angles and down the line. Include chipping, sand shots; pitch shots, and chip shots as well as full swings.

Be incredibly aware that social networking sites, like Facebook, are prime places for coaches to watch you and keep up with you. Any inappropriate posts, photos, comments, etc. are likely to have coaches stop recruiting you before they even begin. Make sure you represent yourself well in these places, because you can be 100% sure coaches are watching you here just as, if not more, critically, as they are on the golf course.

Recognize that coaches who may be about to invest tens of thousands of dollars into you as a student-athlete to represent them, their program, and university, want to make sure the person they select is worth their time, effort, and energy. The cold hard facts are—there are plenty of other student-athletes out there who want the opportunity and are perhaps just as talented, they just need their chance.

A full scholarship at a state school for female golfer, for example, might be in excess of $20,000 per year. If it is awarded each year for four or even five years, the figure reaches $100,000 or more! At private schools the figure could easily be double that amount. If you think coaches want to risk their schools' resources at that level and their careers on someone who can't manage themselves on and off the golf course, you should do some checking.

NOTES

Conducting Team Practices

How to Conduct a Team Practice

Conducting a quality team practice is the single most important thing a coach can do to improve his or her team. Most coaches are familiar with the areas that their teams need to improve, but aren't sure what to do to make these improvements happen.

How to Assess a Team's Skills

Before we can talk about how to conduct a team practice, we must first discuss how to find out what your team needs to improve. The obvious result of a quality practice is to help your players improve their skills which will lead to lower scores in golf tournaments. But, how do you identify what skills your players need to improve? Are all your players at the exact same skill level in all the areas of the game? The answers to these questions can be solved by having your players participate in a series of skills tests before and during tournament season. Some simple skills tests combined with statistics sheets kept for competitive rounds will give you the coach some great insight to how your team plays the game. You will be able to examine exactly where each player excels and each player struggles. This examination is not possible by simply looking at the scorecard after the round. Let's take a look at the skills tests and stat sheets listed below.

Skills Test # 1: The Short Game

Putting	100	95	90	85	80	75	70

3 feet

Beg.	5/5	4/5		3/5	2/5		1/5

10 feet

Beg.	5/5	4/5	3/5	2/5	1/5	2-putt 5/5	

20 feet (2 putt)

Beg.	5/5		4/5		3/5	2/5	1/5

3 ft. ___ + 10 ft. ___ + 20 ft. ___ = ___ /3 = ___

Chipping

Chip from 30' to a 3' radius circle from 2' off the green

	100	95	90	85	80	75	70
Beg.	5/5	4/5		3/5	2/5	1/5	0/5

Pitching

Pitch to a 5' radius circle from 5 yards off the green

	100	95	90	85	80	75	70
Beg.	5/5	4/5		3/5	2/5	1/5	0/5

Sand Play

Hit five shots out of a green-side bunker to a circle with a 10' radius.

100	95	90	85	80	75	70
5/5	4/5	3/5	2/5	1/5	5/5 out	3/5 out

Swing fundamentals

Have students hit 3 shots and count the best two (-10 for each area). For example a good setup with bad posture and bad balance would result in a deduction of 20 points leaving a score of 80. The second swing might show all three fundamentals to be good resulting in a score of 100 while the third showed only one area bad resulting in a score of 90. The best 2 scores, 100 plus 90 would equal 190 divided by 2 would result in a score of 95.

swing 1 swing 2 swing 3

Set up _____ _____ _____

Posture_____ _____ _____   ____ + ____ /2 = _____

Balance_____ _____ _____.

Putting ____ + chipping ___ + pitching ___ + sand play ___ +swing ___ /5= _____ (skills test grade)

Name _____ class_____time _____
skills grade_____

Skills Test #2: The Full Swing

Unless you have unlimited access to a golf course, this skills test must be simulated on a driving range or some sort of practice field. You need to evaluate three areas for junior golfers. The first area is driving. The tee shot sets up the rest of the hole. Getting the ball in play and advancing it a significant distance are keys to driving the ball well.

For the driving test, create a primary target and a surrounding fairway. You can use pre-existing objects like target greens, yardage signs, or trees and other background objects to shape your fairway. You need to also have a method of measuring the total distance of each drive hit. If you do not have a range finder, a close estimation will do.

We will use a simple mathematical formula to come up with a measuring system to compare your players to each other and to players who score within different ranges on the golf course. The formula is:

Total Distance of the Drive – The Number of Yards the Tee Shot Ends Up Away From the Target Line.

Example: Player A hits a drive a distance of 247 yards and 17 yards from the target line. The yardage number of 247 minus the 17 yards the ball was offline equals 230. This is the number you want to track.

The Driving Test

Have each team member hit 10 drives and keep track of the end result of each tee shot using the formula above. Once you have all ten drives recorded, mark a line through the highest number and the lowest number and then average the other eight numbers together. Use the resulting number to compare where your player stands versus others using the chart below.

High School Golfers (Men)

Average Score: 68–78

Average Driving #: 250

Average Score: 78-88

Average Driving #: 230

Average Score: 88-98

Average Driving #: 210

Average Score: 98-108

Average Driving #: 190

Average Score: 108-118

Average Driving #: 170

Average Score: 118+

Average Driving #: 150

Junior High/ Middle School Golfers (Boys)

Average Score: 34-44

Average Driving #: 220

Average Score: 44-54

Average Driving #: 190

Average Score: 54-64

Average Driving #: 160

Average Score: 64+

Average Driving #: 130

Junior high/middle school golfers typically play only nine-hole golf tournaments.

High School Golfers (Women)

Average Score: 68-78

Average Driving #: 220

Average Score: 78-88

Average Driving #: 200

Average Score: 88-98

Average Driving #: 180

Average Score: 98-108

Average Driving #: 160

Average Score: 108-118

Average Driving #: 130

Average Score: 118+

Average Driving #: 100

Junior High/Middle School Golfers (Girls)

Average Score: 34-44

Average Driving #: 190

Average Score: 44-54

Average Driving #: 160

Average Score: 54-64

Average Driving #: 130

Average Score: 64+

Average Driving #: 100

Junior high golfers typically play only nine-hole golf tournaments.

The Driving Test 100–150 Yards

The second area you need to evaluate for your players is from 100 to 150 yards. This is a shot most golfers will face between 7 to 12 times a round. A player's ability to get the ball on the green from this distance is very important to lowering his or her score.

The measurement for this skills test is simple. Have each player hit three shots each hole for nine holes from a different distance within the 100-150 yard range. All that needs to be measured is whether or no the player hit the green in one shot with each ball. Take the total number of shots the player hit on the green in one try and divide that number by 27 (Nine holes played times three shots per hole) and you will come up with a greens in regulation percentage. Use the chart below to see how your players stack up.

High School Golfers (Men)

Average Score: 68-78

Average GIR %: 63

Average Score: 78-88

Average GIR %: 49

Average Score: 88-98

Average GIR%: 35

Average Score: 98-108

Average GIR%: 21

Average Score: 108+

Average GIR%: 7

High School Golfers (Women)

Average Score: 68-78

Average GIR %: 63

Average Score: 78-88

Average GIR %: 49

Average Score: 88-98

Average GIR%: 35

Average Score: 98-108

Average GIR%: 21

Average Score: 108+

Average GIR% #: 7

Junior High Golfers (Boys)

Average Score: 34-44

Average GIR %: 55

Average Score: 44-54

Average GIR %: 35

Average Score: 54-64

Average GIR%: 15

Average Score: 64+

Average GIR%: 5

Junior high golfers typically play only nine-hole golf tournaments.

Junior High Golfers (Girls)

Average Score: 34-44

Average GIR %: 55

Average Score: 44-54

Average GIR %: 35

Average Score: 54-64

Average GIR%: 15

Average Score: 64+

Average GIR%: 5

Junior high golfers typically play only nine-hole golf tournaments.

The Driving Test 30–100 Yards

The third area you need to evaluate for your players is from 30 to 100 yards. This is a shot most golfers will face between 12 to 18 times a round. A player's ability to get the ball on the green and close to the hole from this distance is very important to lowering his or her score.

The measurement for this skills test is simple. Have each player hit three shots each hole for nine holes from a different distance within the 30 to 100 yard range. All that needs to be measured is the distance from the hole the player hit each ball. Each player will need some form of measuring device to complete this exercise. A tape measure or a long piece of yarn should do the trick. Balls hit that do not end up on the green can have their distance from the hole estimated. Use the chart below to see how your players stack up.

High School Golfers (Men)

Average Score: 68-78

Average Proximity: 15 ft.

Average Score: 78-88

Average Proximity: 25 ft.

Average Score: 88-98

Average Proximity: 45 ft.

Average Score: 98-108

Average Proximity: 65 ft.

Average Score: 108+

Average Proximity: 85 ft.

High School Golfers (Women)

Average Score: 68-78

Average Proximity: 15 ft.

Average Score: 78-88

Average Proximity: 25 ft.

Average Score: 88-98

Average Proximity: 45 ft.

Average Score: 98-108

Average Proximity: 65 ft.

Average Score: 108+

Average Proximity: 85 ft.

Junior High Golfers (Boys)

Average Score: 34-44

Average Proximity: 20 ft.

Average Score: 44-54

Average Proximity: 40 ft.

Average Score: 54-64

Average Proximity: 60 ft.

Average Score: 64+

Average Proximity: 90 ft.

Junior high golfers typically play only nine-hole golf tournaments.

Junior High Golfers (Girls)

Average Score: 34-44

Average Proximity: 20 ft.

Average Score: 44-54

Average Proximity: 40 ft.

Average Score: 54-64

Average Proximity: 60 ft.

Average Score: 64+

Average Proximity: 90 ft.

Junior high golfers typically only play nine-hole golf tournaments.

These three skills tests are the best way to measure the skills of your team members in a practice setting. However, some players perform differently in tournament situations. Because this is the case, you should require your players to complete stat sheets after every competitive round. While statistics don't always show the whole picture, they give you a great insight into how each player performs in the important areas of the game.

Please see the resource section of this book for tournament stat sheets.

The Elements of a Quality Team Practice

Now that you know how to measure your players' strengths and weaknesses, we can talk about how to conduct a quality team practice. Conducting a quality practice requires several elements to be in place. Let's discuss some of these elements.

Punctuality

It is important that all players are required to be on time to practice. This signals to all team members that no one player is more important than another. Set a specific time frame for each practice and hold players accountable for not abiding by it.

Purpose

Each practice should have a specific purpose. That purpose should be communicated to the players before and during each practice. It is the coach's job to make sure the players are staying focused and on task.

Drills

When you set out to help your team improve through practice, identifying the weaknesses to work on is only half the game. You must put practice drills and situations in place to help your players work on any deficiencies they have. Please see the resources section and the drills DVD for various practice drills to use.

Forward Looking

Improving upon each team member's skills is important. However, a coach must balance improving his team's skills and getting his team in the proper mindset to compete in a golf tournament. Look at your season tournament schedule and try to work on your skills before and in between golf tournaments. The closer your team gets to a tournament date, the more time should be spent on the golf course getting them ready to play.

Closed

Practices are for coaches and team members. We strongly advise you to keep the player's parents out of your practices. Encourage them to watch, but inform them that they are not allowed to participate in any way. Let them know that you will be happy to answer any questions they may have after practice or in another setting.

YOUR BIGGEST INFLUENCE ON YOUR PLAYERS WILL BE IN PRACTICE SETTINGS. STATE JUNIOR GOLF RULES ALLOW ALMOST ZERO CONTACT WITH YOUR PLAYERS ONCE A TOURNAMENT ROUND BEGINS. PREPARE YOUR PLAYERS PROPERLY FOR EACH TOURNAMENT AND THEN STEP OUT OF THE WAY AND LET THEM PLAY.

Organizing and Conducting Team Qualifying

How to Conduct a Qualifying

Now that you have taught your team how to practice and what to practice, it's time to measure their abilities in a competitive situation. The ultimate test of a golfer's skill is the scores he or she shoots in tournaments. Unfortunately, you can't afford to take your entire golf team to every tournament. This puts you the coach in a tough situation. Who are your best players? Will all your players perform equally well on different golf courses? Who is the most ready to compete in a tournament now? Who should be given special consideration when they aren't playing their best?

These are all questions you must be able to answer to ensure that you are bringing your best team to every tournament. There is only one way for you to answer all of these questions, and that is by conducting qualifying rounds for each tournament. Most golf tournaments allow you to bring up to five players. Your qualifying methods must help you choose your five best players out of a squad that could have as many as fifteen players. Let's take a look at how to conduct fair and effective qualifying rounds.

Plan Your Qualifying Methods and Stick to Your Plan

There are many different ways to conduct a qualifying process. The key for any coach is to choose a method and to stick with it through thick and thin. Let's examine some qualifying methods.

The Low Score Method

Each player plays a predetermined number of holes on the same golf course, and the scores are totaled. The players with the five lowest scores will travel to the tournament. You need to have your players play at least 27 holes for this to be an accurate method.

Pros:

> This method keeps your players practicing and on their toes. They cannot afford a bad performance or they will be left at home.
>
> This method allows the coach to avoid the appearance of bias towards any single player. The lowest scores advance. The coach has no say.

Cons:

> This method requires that you play at least 27 holes of qualifying to be effective. For golfers in school, this means you will need at least three days of practice to complete this method.
>
> If one of your better players plays poorly, you have no means by which to take him to the tournament. Golf is a sport in which any player can have a bad day. For example your number one player all year is sick and plays poorly in the qualifier for the state golf tournament. He finishes sixth in qualifying play. This method does not allow you to take his past performance into account when forming your team.

The Low Score/Pick Method

This method allows you to conduct a combination qualifier. You will have a predetermined number of spots that will be won by the lowest score. You will also have a number of spots that you the coach will pick to go to the tournament even if one person's score is lower than the other. The minimum number of holes to be played for this method is 18. This is the recommended method of the authors of this book.

Pros:

> This method requires only 18 holes to be played for it to be effective. This means that you can complete your qualifying play in as little as two practices.
>
> This method allows you to reward players on things other than just the lowest score. Hard work, punctuality, good attitude, and other things can be taken into consideration when forming your team. The coach's ability to pick a certain number of players helps you avoid having to leave one of your better players at home. If a player has a bad day, you can use your coach's pick to take him to the tournament.

Cons:

> This method can make the coach appear to have a bias towards a player or players. You must have some empirical data that you can show to parents

and possibly administrators that support why you selected a child with higher scores over a child with lower scores. You can back up your decision with past qualifying scores, tournament results, practice attendance, academic success, and other measurements. Keeping accurate records of these things can help you.

Your better players may not practice and compete as hard in qualifying because they think that you will pick them to go to the tournament no matter what they do. Treat all of your players as equals and this mindset will not occur.

The Ladder System

The ladder system is a qualifying method in which you have your players play at least 36 holes of qualifying. You then take their scores and rank each player from first to last by lowest score to highest score. The only way for a player to change his ranking is for him to challenge the player ranked directly above him, or to be challenged by the player directly below him. A player can advance or lose a position only by winning or losing a match. Your top five players will go to each tournament.

Pros:

> You get to see your players play a lot of golf because this method requires 36 holes of play to be effective.

Players continually have to challenge and be challenged to maintain or advance their place on the team pecking order.

Cons:

You will need at least four practices to complete the 36 holes of qualifying play.

If a player plays way above or below his skill level in the ranking round, he may find it hard to move up the ladder, or you the coach may find it hard to move him down the ladder.

A feeling of hopelessness can take over the players on the bottom of the ladder and a feeling of arrogance can take over the players at the top of the ladder.

A Few Tips for Any Qualifying Method

Put your qualifying method in writing and hand it out to your players and parents at the beginning of the season. Remember, it's ok to combine qualifying methods. For example you use the low score method for the regular season, but once the post season begins you switch to the low score/pick method. Make sure your methods are very clear from the start of the season.

Do your absolute best to make sure all players qualify on the same golf course on the same days. The difficulty of one golf course versus another cannot be accurately measured. Also, the weather conditions of one day may not be the same as another.

Hold your players accountable for getting to qualifying rounds and completing them as scheduled.

Change the way you pair your players. This helps guard against any cheating accusations, and makes your team compete more seriously.

Establish the rules for each qualifying round before it starts. Try to simulate tournament rules.

Set up the golf course you normally play to represent the course you will play in your next tournament. For example your golf course is 7400 yards long and wide open off of the tee. Your next tournament is on a golf course that is 6000 yards long and very narrow off of the tee. Play for a yardage that simulates the course you will play in your next event.

Keeping Stats

Practice Logs and Useful Forms

Stat Sheets

Keeping stats is an extremely accurate way of identifying ones strengths and weaknesses, as well as tracking ones progress. The stat sheet, when kept properly, provides valuable unbiased information for the coach as well as the player. It can help players and coaches determine where and what type of practice will be the most beneficial. Good players are always aware of their stats.

When keeping stats it is imperative that they are kept accurately. For example if a player putts from off the green it is considered a chip and does not count as a putt. The following stat sheet is simple and easy to keep and should be filled out immediately following the round. An argument can be made that a player cannot remember what he or she did on a hole especially if they are a beginner. It is still important that they begin the process so as to make it a habit as their game progresses.

Practice Forms

A practice log is also a good way of making sure you are focused during your practice session. During the practice session review your purpose and key thoughts before you start. Write down the drills you are going to be doing and keep notes on how the session goes. Write down feelings that you had during the session, good and bad, as well as the results.

Player: _____

Tournament: _____

Date: _____ Course: _____

Par: _____ Score: _____

Tees: _____ Yardage: _____

Hole	1	2	3	4	5	6	7	8	9	Out
Par										
Score										
Fwy										
Green										
Putts										
U/I										
Sand										

"Relax and Have Fun"

Hole	10	11	12	13	14	15	16	17	18	In	Tot
Par											
Score											
Fwy											
Green											
Putts											
U/I											
Sand											

Scoring

Pars:		Birdies:		Eagles:	
Bogies:		Dbl. Bogies:		Other:	

Pars or better Vs. - Par 3's		Par 4's		Par 5's	

Putting

Total Putts:		1-Putt:		2-Putt:		3-Putt:		Other:

Driving Fairways Hit (in regulations): _____

Approach Greens (in regulation): _____

Short Game

Up and In's (for par or better): _____

Sand up and In's (for par or better): _____

Golfers Practice Log

Date _____ Place _____ Time _____ to _____

Practice session

Purpose _____

Key thoughts _____

Drills

_____

_____

_____

Notes

_____

_____

_____

_____

_____

_____

_____

_____

_____

_____

_____

_____

_____

_____

_____

_____

_____

_____

_____

Developing Junior Programs

Junior golf is more than just young people playing golf. Junior golf is young people learning responsibility, honesty, integrity, confidence, respect, and the benefits of hard work, not to mention a lifelong sport, as well as many other qualities that will help them throughout their lives. From the time I started my first junior program in 1986 until now we have had over 400 kids go to college on some type of scholarship and play golf. We have had 9 students become PGA professionals, 29 win state titles, and 30 teams win state championships. More importantly we helped to make golf a part of a lot of people's lives and that is why many of our students today are kids of students we taught years ago.

Starting a junior program is simple really. You need to provide juniors with three things;

Equipment
An opportunity to learn (year round)
An opportunity to play

All three areas are equally important. Many junior programs fail to become productive due to the organizers lack of understanding of the importance of instruction on a regular basis and **PLAYING OPPORTUNITIES**. If juniors do not have an opportunity to play and at some point compete the program will fail.

Equipment

It's pretty easy to get equipment for juniors. Visit local facilities and ask them for their old demo irons and put a sign up in the golf shops asking for old clubs that can be used for junior golf. You can also contact the PGA section in your area and they will be more than happy to help.

Instruction

Providing opportunities for juniors to learn on a regular basis is a must. A clinic twice a year even with Tiger Woods as a guest will do little to keep juniors interested in learning to play golf. Weekly instruction is the key to successful junior programs. All that is needed is a golf facility that's willing to allow you some time on the range and or the short game area one day per week. If this is absolutely not a possibility then a gym or playground at a local school will work. Start by scheduling some time weekly for some basic instruction. We recommend you split the ages up as follows; 10 and under, 11–13, and 14 and up. Be flexible enough to allow a 9-year-old who is advanced to attend class with the 11–13 year olds. Saturday mornings or afternoons work best. Weekday afternoons often cause problems for juniors. It sometimes is difficult for parents to make transportation arrangements in the afternoon due to conflicts with their work schedules. We have classes every Saturday; a 9am class for the 10 and under, a 10 am class for the 11–13 age group, and a 11 am class for the 14 and up age group. We also provide an afterschool program for those who can make it on Mondays and Wednesdays. This book provides all that's needed to conduct classes on a weekly basis. Visit www.texasjuniorgolf.org to see our other programs and feel free to contact us at hotgolfinc@sbcglobal.net for help in starting a junior program.

Playing Opportunities

Playing opportunities is perhaps the most important element in a successful junior program. Learning golf can be fun but not nearly as much fun as actually playing golf. Kids want to play once they begin the learning process and should be encouraged to do so as often as possible. Some organizers believe that juniors should almost master the game before attempting to play. That belief is far from correct. Juniors who play while taking lessons will progress much faster than those who do not and have a higher rate of continuing to play the game for years to come. We recommend a Parent-Child tournament once a month if possible. This format allows very young juniors to get out on the course with their parents. We usually put a couple of juniors and a couple of parents on each team and have them play a 4-person scramble, usually from the 150-yard marker on each hole, for 9 holes. This allows beginners to hit every shot yet not have to play their shot the entire hole, saving time and frustration while learning. Depending on the facility this tournament may have to be held late in the day on Saturday or Sunday during non peak hours.

When utilizing a gym or a field the process is a bit more challenging. Wiffle balls or tennis balls and mats are required and creativity is a must. SNAG Golf makes some great equipment for indoor use along with an instructional video on how to utilize it. When indoors remember that **safety** comes first.

Junior programs are beneficial to everyone remotely involved in the golf industry as well as to the success of local school programs. A successful junior program will result in more members at the local golf courses, more equipment sales, more private lessons, more activity at the golf course snack bar or restaurant and definitely a more successful school program. We began our programs in 1986 in Waco and since that time 31 area schools have won state championships!!!

Conducting Junior Events

People do not care how much you know until they know how much you care. Everyone has heard that saying. Remember in junior golf there is always a parent, grandparent or friend helping that junior golfer get started in golf. For many people you are their first impression of competitive golf. Make the event as friendly and fun as possible for both the youngster and the parent.

Organizing a Tournament

Advertise early for maximum exposure: TV, radio, newspaper, online, at the golf courses, schools, with coaches. Be sure your entry blank has all of the details necessary: starting times, age groups, eligibility, entry fee, and contact information, phone and email. Prior to the event be sure that you have thoroughly coordinated with the golf course on the location of a sign-in area; scoreboards, cart use by tournament staff, and any items that the course will provide, such as food, range balls, or score sheets, for example.

Day of the Event

Be at the course early! Post all rules on the scoreboard and at the sign-in area and have copies available for the players and tournament staff. Post all policies concerning parent and spectator involvement (e.g. advice, caddying, etc.). Encourage all fans and players to abide by USGA Rules—this simplifies everything. Have a current rule book and decisions book and the USGA 1-800 number on hand. Be ready to answer all questions concerning range finders, carts, pull carts, caddies advice—these are best answered by having your rules policies posted BEFORE the tournament begins. Have a clear policy for weather challenges—lightning, rain, delayed play, cancelled play and evacuating players from the course.

Staffing

Have plenty of staff available to tee off players, handle rules decisions, man the scoreboard, help transporting players on and off the course in weather situations,and present trophies, as well as a person in charge of contacting the media with tournament results.

FINALLY: Smile, relax, and enjoy the kids.

Structure and Timing

Running the event efficiently is a must. We want the facility to be out as little as possible. Having junior events usually costs the facility money since juniors pay a lower green fee and must walk as opposed to riding a golf cart. Below is an example of how we structure our junior events. This format allows the course to reopen to the public in the quickest manner and is far better than a shotgun-type event.

There are four age groups for the boys and four age groups for the girls, 10 & under, 11–12, 13–14, and 15–18.
Medals are awarded for first, second, & third place in each age group.

We tee the 15–-18 boys off the number 1 tee with tee-times beginning at 8:30 followed by the 13–14 age boys the 15–18 age girls and finally the 13–14 age girls. All these groups play 18 holes. The 15–18 boys play from the back tees, the 13–14 boys play from the middle tees, and the girls play from the front tees. At the same time we tee the 11–12 boys off the tenth tee with tee-times beginning at 8:30 followed by the 11–12 year old girls. Both these groups play 9 holes. The 10 and under boys and girls begin play on hole 13 with tee-times beginning at 8:30. This group plays 6 holes from the 200 yard marker on par 4's and 5's and from the front tees on par 3's.

The above system allows the course to reopen for regular play after the last tee time on the front, for most events usually around 10:30 to 11:00.

It is our recommendation that you keep the event as inexpensive as possible, thereby ensuring that juniors of all economic backgrounds are able to participate. Try to find local sponsors to help pay for the medals, thus helping to keep the cost down. If you can schedule the event on a day when the course is normally closed or on a day that is slow for the facility the fee charged by the facility for each junior is usually lower. The event is an excellent opportunity to give a rules clinic before or after the competition as well as to share information with the juniors about upcoming camps, clinics, and playing opportunities.

GLOSSARY

Ace: A hole completed in one stroke.

Address: The process that a player goes through in positioning himself and the club or a stroke.

Approach Shot: A full stroke played to the putting green, usually made with a medium or short iron.

Apron: The bordering grass around the green, not as short as the green but usually shorter than the fairway. Sometimes called the "fringe."

Away: The ball deemed farthest from the hole, to be played first.

Back Door: A description for a putt that rolls around the cup and falls in from the rear.

Back Nine: The second nine holes of an eighteen-hole golf course.

Backspin: A reverse spin imparted to the ball, which causes it to stop quickly upon landing.

Banana Ball: A slang term for a shot that curves wildly from left to right.

Best Ball:	A match in which one golfer plays against the better ball of two players or the best ball of three players.
Birdie:	A score of one stroke under par for a hole.
Bite:	Backspin imparted to the ball, which makes it stop abruptly.
Blade:	Description of a putter with a thin head.
Bogey:	A score of one stroke over par on a hole.
Brassie:	The #2 wood. Seldom included in a matched set of clubs today.
Break of Green:	The slant or the slope of the green, sometimes called "borrow," when considering the amount of curve to allow for.
Bunker:	A hazard or a depressed area filled with sand. In common usage called a sand trap.
Caddie:	Someone who carries a player's clubs. A caddie may give advice to the player.
Carry:	The distance that a ball travels in the air before striking the ground.

Casual Water: An accumulation of water which is temporary. Not considered a water hazard.

Chip Shot: A short and usually low-trajectory shot played to the green.

Closed Face: One in which the face of the club points to the left of the intended line of flight.

Closed Stance: The left foot is closer to the intended line of flight than the right foot.

Clubface: The normal striking surface of the head of the club.

Course Rating: The difficulty rating of a course assigned by a committee which uses guidelines provided by the United States Golf Association.

Couey Corollary: Named for Dick Couey who hated to make, and usually missed, short putts. His fellow players allowed him to pick up short putts that were **within**, or even **touched**, the putter's grip.

Cup: The metal lining of the hole on the putting green. It is 4 1/4" in diameter and at least 4" deep.

Cut Shot: A stroke that gives the ball a clockwise spin and causes it to curve from left to right.

Divot: A piece of turf which is displaced by a player's club. It should be replaced and patted down, or filled in with sand and seed.

Dogleg: A hole with a fairway that bends to the right or to the left.

Dormie: A situation in match play in which a player or a team is leading by as many holes as there are holes remaining.

Double Bogey: A score of two strokes over par on a hole.

Double Eagle: A score of three strokes under par on a hole.

Down: The number of holes a player or a side is behind in a match.

Draw: A shot which curves slightly to the left.

Drive: A shot made from the teeing ground.

Driver: The #1 wood or metal club.

Dub: A poorly hit shot.

Duffer: A poor golfer. Also sometimes called a "hacker."

Eagle: A score of two strokes under par on a hole.

Explosion Shot: A shot from a sand bunker in which the club head slides under the ball and displaces a fairly large amount of sand.

Fade: A shot which curves slightly to the right.

Fairway: The mowed area of the golf course between the teeing ground and the putting green.

Fat Shot: A stroke in which the ground is struck before the ball.

Flag or flagstick: The movable pole in the hole with a flag attached to the top. Also called the pin.

Flat Swing: A swing that is less upright and more shallow than the normal swing.

Flight: The path that the ball takes in the air; or a division of players in a tournament according to playing ability.

Follow-Through: The part of the swing after the club face has contacted the ball.

Fore: A warning which is shouted to anyone in danger of being hit by a golf ball.

Foursome: The common term for four players playing in a group.

Forward Press: A slight movement toward the target of some part of the body prior to the backswing.

Frog Hair: Same as apron.

Gimmie: A slang expression for a conceded putt in match plays.

Grain: The direction in which flat-lying grass grows on a putting green.

Grip: The upper portion of the club shaft. Also the player's grasp of the club.

Gross Score: The player's actual score on a hole or a round, with no handicap strokes deducted.

Ground: Touching the ground with the sole of the club at address. This is not allowed in a hazard.

Ground Under Repair: Designated areas on a golf course that allow for free drop outside those areas.

Halved: A term used to designate a tied hole in match play.

Handicap: A number which indicates a golfer's skill. It is based upon the difference between the actual scores a player shoots and the course ratings of the courses on which the scores were made. It provides a way for players of different abilities to play on a fairly equal basis.

Hazard: According to the United States Golf Association rules, a designation for a bunker (sand trap, water area, or water hazard.

Head: The striking part of the club at the lower end of the shaft.

Heeled Shot: A shot hit near or off the portion of the club that attaches to the shaft.

High Side:	The area above the hole on a sloping green.
Hole Out:	To stroke the ball into the cup.
Honor:	The privilege of shooting first from the teeing ground.
Hood:	A closed club face. Tilting the top edge of the club forward, thus decreasing the loft.
Hook:	A shot that curves in flight from right to left.
Hosel:	The extension of the head of the club into which the shaft fits.
In:	The designation on a score card for the second nine holes of an eighteen-hole course.
Inside-Out:	The club head moves across the intended line of flight from left to right during impact.
Interlock Grip:	A type of grip in which the left forefinger and right little finger are intertwined.
LPGA:	The Ladies Professional Golf Association.

Lag: Putting with the intention of ending close to the hole.

Lateral Water Hazard:

A water hazard that runs parallel or almost parallel to the line of play on a hole.

Lie: The position of the ball on the course. Also refers to the angle formed by the sole of the club and the shaft.

Links: A term that refers to, that which is built over sandy soil deposited by ocean tides ("linked to the seas"). Today a term used synonymously with golf course.

Lip: The edge of the hole. Also a putt that rims the hole but does not go in.

Loft of the Club: The backward slant or angle of the club face. Also, to cause the ball to rise into the air.

Loose Impediment: A natural object not fixed or growing, such as pebbles, leaves, and twigs.

Low Side: The area below the hole on a slanted green.

Mashie: A hickory-shafted iron club similar the current 5-iron.

Match Play: Competition based on the number of holes won or lost rather than on strokes.

Medal: The lowest of all of the qualifying scores. The person shooting this score is the medalist

Mulligan: In friendly competition, an illegal second shot from the first tee if the first shot is a poor one. Named after a Canadian, Dr. David Mulligan.

Nassau: A type of scoring in which three points are given: one for each nine holes and one for the eighteen holes.

Net Score: The score for a hole or for a round after the player's handicap has been deducted from the gross score.

Niblick: A club somewhat like the current 9-iron.

Obstruction: Usually refers to anything on the course that is artificial, whether fixed, or movable. See USGA rules for exceptions.

Open Face: The club head is aimed right of the intended line of flight.

Open Stance: The right foot is closer than the left foot to the intended line of flight.

Open Tournament: Competition that allows the entry of both amateurs and professionals.

Out Of Bounds: An area usually marked by stakes, a fence, or a wall, which is outside of the course proper. Play in this area is prohibited.

Out: The designation for the first nine holes of an eighteen-hole course, or designating which golfer is away from the hole.

Outside-In: Movement of the club head from right to left across the intended line of flight.

Overlap or Overlapping:

                       The grip in which the right little finger laps over the left forefinger.

Par: The score a skilled player is expected to move on a hole. This score allows for two putts.

PGA: The men's Professional Golf Association of America. The PGA was founded in 1916.

Pitch Shot: An approach shot with a high trajectory, which stops relatively fast after landing.

Play Through: An invitation given by slower players to let the group behind them go ahead.

Preferred Lie: An easing of the rules that permits the players to move the ball to a better position in the fairway when course conditions are poor. Also called "winter rules."

Provisional Ball: A second ball that is hit before a player looks for an original ball which might be lost or out-of-bounds.

Press: Using more force than necessary or attempting to stroke beyond one's own ability; or doubling the original bet in wagering for the remaining holes.

Pull Shot: A shot that travels on a fairly straight line to the left of the intended target.

Push: A shot that travels on a fairly straight line to the right of the intended target.

Putter: The least-lofted club, which is usually used only on the putting green.

Rough: An area that has fairly long grass. It is not considered fairway, hazard, or green.

Rub Of The Green: A term used for the situation in which a shot is stopped or deflected by an outside agency.

Sand Wedge: A club with a heavy, wide sole that is designed principally to be used in sand bunkers.

Scotch Foursome: Common term for a foursome in which two teams compete, each team using only one ball and hitting it alternately.

Scrambler: A player who shows exceptional skills around the green after demonstrating loose play in getting there. In other words, a slang expression for a player who can get the ball up and in the hole from out of a garbage can.

Scratch Player: A player who has a handicap of zero and who plays consistently close to par.

Shanking: Hitting the ball with the neck of the club, making it travel in an oblique direction to the right.

Skying: Hitting the ball high in the air only a short distance, when it was intended to travel much farther.

Slice: A shot that curves sharply from left to right of the intended line of flight.

Sole: The bottom of the club head.

Spoon: The #3 wood.

Square Stance: A stance in which a line drawn from the toe of the right foot to the toe of the left foot runs parallel to the line of flight.

Square Face: The club head is aimed at the intended line of flight at the address.

Stiff: A shot that finished very close to the flagstick.

Stroke Play: Competition based upon the total strokes taken by a player or a side.

Sudden Death: Extra holes played by players tied at the end of competition until a winner is determined.

Summer Rules: The official rules of golf that require the player to play the ball as it lie.

Takeaway: The initial part of the backswing.

Target Line: The imaginary line that extends from the player's target back to, through, and beyond the ball.

Tee: The small wooden peg from which the ball is played on the teeing ground.

Teeing Ground: A rectangular area defined by markers, which is no more than two club lengths in depth. The first shot of every hole is played from here and is commonly called the "tee".

Tee Markers: The markers placed on the teeing ground that designate the point from which play of the hole begins.

Texas Wedge: A slang term that refers to the putter when it is used for shots from off the putting green.

Through The Green: A designation for the whole area of the course except the teeing ground and the green of the hole being played, and including all hazards.

Tight Lie: A ball that is well down in the grass or very close to the surface being played.

Toed Shot: A shot that is struck on or near the toe of the club.

Topped Shot: A rolling or low bounding shot that is caused by striking the ball above its center of gravity.

Unplayable Lie: A ball (not in a water hazard) that is determined to be unplayable by its owner.

USGA: The United States Golf Association, the governing body of golf in the United States. Organized in 1894.

Waggle: Club head movement at the time of address and prior to the swing.

Whiff: A miss. A stroke in which no contact is made with the ball.

Winter Rules: A situation in which the course is not in top playable condition; therefore a player is allowed to improve the lie of his/her ball.